# AMAZONIA

# AMAZONIA

PHOTOGRAPHS AND TEXT BY
## Loren McIntyre

Sierra Club Books

SAN FRANCISCO

LIBRARY OF CONGRESS CATALOGING-IN-PUBLICATION DATA

McIntyre, Loren, 1917–
    Amazonia / Loren McIntyre.
      p.  cm.
    Includes index.
    ISBN 0-87156-641-9
     1. Amazon River Valley—Description and travel.   2. Amazon River Valley—Description and travel—Views.   3. Natural history—Amazon River Valley.   I. Title.
F2546.M5  1991
918.1′1—dc20
                                         91-6573
                                           CIP

EDITOR: David Spinner
PRODUCTION: Susan Ristow
BOOK AND JACKET DESIGN: Paula Schlosser
MAP: Earth Surface Graphics
COMPOSITION: Wilsted & Taylor

PRINTED AND BOUND IN TOKYO BY TOPPAN PRINTING COMPANY, LTD.

10   9   8   7   6   5   4   3   2   1

TO CHICHI'S COUSINS IN THE CANOPY.
*QUE VIVAN!*

# CONTENTS

# FOREWORD

A FASCINATION WITH THE Amazon and with rainforests in general is so deeply imbedded in our culture that many people come to love these places almost unconsciously. Most North Americans have never been in the presence of any of the world's rainforests, and yet the frequent concern they express for the forests' well-being reveals a deep well of feeling and support for these marvelous places. That feeling can be harnessed usefully only if we increase our understanding of rainforests, of what they are and how and why they are threatened. This beautiful book is a good place to start.

In the first instance, it is the beauty of Amazonia that makes us care about its fate. Loren McIntyre captures that beauty and expands on it for us, showing not only the animals, plants, rivers, and people of Amazonia, but also the feeling, the light and shadow of the place, with the understanding gained during his many years of travel there. Amazonia is not a single item, not a unity. It is many different landscapes, nations, habitats, colors, smells, moods, and lessons. No one person can see it all, but Loren McIntyre has seen a great deal of it: we are privileged to have a glimpse of it through his eyes.

Looking at these pictures, one is struck by Amazonia's capacity to astonish. There is, too, something about Amazonia that encourages myth-making. Even today, travellers often feel that a mere recounting of the facts does not adequately convey their sense of what it was like to be there. It seems necessary to exaggerate in order to tell the truth. Myths have an important place in the history of the Amazon. The very name *Amazon* comes from tales told by the Spanish explorer Francisco de Orellana of encounters with a tribe of fierce female warriors during his descent of the river in 1541. Soon afterward, the mysterious forest became famous as the reputed site of *El Dorado*, the Gilded Man and the legendary land of gold. Here are the seeds of two myths—that the Amazon is peopled by warlike primitive tribes and that it is a place of fabulous wealth—that are still at the heart of our misapprehension and mistreatment of Amazonia.

The Amazon has always attracted adventurers, speculators, and those who can afford to dream on a large scale. Among the many mega-schemes that have been tried in the Amazon was Fordlandia, Henry Ford's money-losing attempt during the 1930s to create the world's largest rubber plantation. After sinking millions of dollars into it, Ford was finally defeated by labor problems and by leaf blight fungus. In 1982, Daniel Ludwig, at one time the richest man in the world, washed his hands of the Jarí project in the Brazilian Amazon after having spent more than a billion dollars in an effort to establish a paper pulp mill.

The latest, and by the far the largest, assault on the Amazon Basin is Brazil's Grande Carajas project, a multibillion-dollar regional development scheme funded by the World Bank, other development agencies, and many private foreign and Brazilian banks and companies. Grande Carajas extends over an area the size of Great Britain and France combined, a place that is home to more than 12,000 Indians and more than 20 Indian reserves. Among the developments planned or already under way are the world's largest iron mine and other mines for gold, copper, manganese, nickel, and tin; the fourth largest dam in the world; a 900-kilometer-long electric railway; a deepwater port; several pig iron smelters to be fueled with charcoal made from trees cut from virgin rainforest; a chemical fertilizer plant; a sawmill; 300 cattle ranches; 2 huge colonization projects; and 10 new cities. One of the subschemes calls for clearcutting 10,000 square miles of forest.

The trouble with these types of plan is that they are based on misconceptions about the forest. Amazonia delights in disguises. Almost nothing there is as it seems. It is not, as it has often been painted, an unconquerable, exuberantly fertile land, whose treasures, guarded by a few primitive savages, are waiting to be exploited.

Amazonia is the largest tropical rainforest in the world, but it is not unconquerable. Originally, more than 2 million square miles of the region were covered by dense tropical forest. For centuries, its vastness and inaccessibility have protected the preponderant part of the forest, and still do so today. However, over the past 30 years, government-sponsored road-building projects, colonization schemes, and industrial developments have transformed large areas of Amazonia from pristine forest to polluted factory sites and sprawling settlements. This is proof that we can destroy this great forest and an ominous harbinger of things to come as the heavily exploited rainforests of Africa and Southeast Asia run out.

The abundant life that strikes visitors to the Amazon rainforest exists not in one of the most fertile environments on Earth, but in one of the most hostile. Amazonia is characterized by constant high temperatures, frequent and intense rainfall, and some of the poorest soils in the world. The forest itself moderates these difficult conditions: its extensive canopy provides shade and a cushion against erosive rains; its massive root system stores water during the rainy season and releases it gradually throughout the rest of the year; and the leaves, twigs, and branches that litter the forest floor provide nutrients for growing plants.

So successfully has the rainforest overcome its limitations that most visitors have been fooled. They have misread adaptation for boundless fecundity. The great Victorian naturalist Henry Bates announced that "every inch of [its] soil is of the most exuberant fertility." His sometime travelling companion, Alfred Wallace, was equally unrealistic, writing, "When I consider the excessively small amount of labour required in this country, to convert the virgin forest into green meadows and fertile plantations, I almost long to come over with half-a-dozen friends, disposed to work, and enjoy the country; and show the inhabitants how soon an earthly paradise might be created."

Wallace's comment illustrates a third highly damaging myth about the Amazon: that it is underpopulated and that those who do live there are primitive savages who have not made good use of the resources at their disposal. Though the sophistication and skill of the people of the rainforest as hunters and gatherers have long been acknowledged, their skills as farmers are still seriously underrated by most agronomists. Modern Western farmers have powerful tools that in effect homogenize the land, enabling them to plant and tend vast fields of a single crop. So-called primitive farmers, however, rely on skills, not on tools. The more "primitive" a farming system is, the more knowledgeable and skillful the farmer must be. Forest farmers create in the fields a complex replica of the forest—with all its diversity, its layers of trees, shrubs, and herbs, its mixture of plants and animals.

Only 6 percent of the soils in the Amazon Basin have no major limitations for agriculture, and these are scattered throughout the region. The Indians know how to find and successfully work these isolated pockets of fertility. Proof of this abounds but is almost universally ignored by planners and politicians. A study by Emilio Moran, an agricultural and ecological anthropologist at Indiana University, found that settlers imported into the Brazilian Amazon in the early 1970s on a government colonization scheme invariably chose to establish their farms where the trees were thick-trunked and gave the impression of vigorous growth. In fact, these areas were always associated with the typical nutrient-poor soils of the rainforest. Traditional shifting cultivators in the area, however, looked for certain thin-trunked species, which, scientists later discovered, indicated well-drained, clay-rich soils. The local shift cultivators—farmers who practice field rather than crop rotation—also grew a different mixture of crops. After one year of farming, the soil of the native farms proved to have superior chemical composition to that of the newcomers in every respect. The native farm income was twice that of the settlers, despite the settlers' access to government agricultural advisors.

The people of the forest know most about how the forest works. They know hundreds of edible, medicinal, and poisonous plants. Researchers believe that the greenheart tree, which has a reputation in the Amazon as an effective contraceptive, has medical potential. Botanists say that there are probably many species of flowering plants in South America that local people know and use but that are as yet unknown to scientists.

Attempts by people of the rainforest to defend their lands against invasion have been distorted into a myth of their savagery. On the contrary, some among the invaders have proved themselves masters of cruelty, both physical and psychological. Some anthropologists estimate, according to a World Bank report in 1982, that in 1500 the Amazon Basin had a thriving population of from 6 to 9 million. By 1900, Brazil, the major part of Amazonia, had only 1 million Indians. Today Brazil has fewer than 200,000 Indians. About half of the 230 tribes in Brazil at the turn of the century are extinct. This extinction has not been solely a result of warfare or direct attacks. According to investigations by agencies as diverse as the human rights group Survival International and the Brazilian government, tens of thousands of Indians have died after being infected—sometimes in deliberate acts of genocide—by diseases for which they have no resistance and no medicine.

The most damaging and tenacious myth is the idea that if the rainforest is not exploited its treasures will go to waste. It is often claimed that rainforests must be sacrificed for the betterment of the poor and the landless, but the effect of most rainforest exploitation is to redistribute wealth upward. The permanent, wide-reaching benefits of the intact forest—the protection of wildlife, water catchments, soil, and a stable global climate; and the provision of food, medicines, and building materials—are sacrificed for short-term profits for a small group of investors and consumers. The rest of the world—those who live in Amazonia and those who do not—are the poorer for it.

Rainforests are not empty, underutilized lands whose true value will only be realized when they are replaced by logging operations, agricultural colonies, cattle ranches, mines, or hydroelectric dams. The rainforest is not in general suitable for conventional agriculture or for large-scale settlements. Small groups of people already live wherever the forest can support human life, and millions of people who live outside the rainforest depend on its remaining intact. The rainforest protects the soil and regulates the flow of rivers in land far beyond its own borders. Up to half of all rainfall in the Amazon Basin comes from water evaporated from the forest itself. Deforestation disrupts that cycle, reducing rainfall locally, and the burning or decomposition of felled trees adds carbon to the atmosphere and intensifies the greenhouse effect, the cause of global warming. Rainforests also support the richest biological community on Earth, the source of many of the world's most important crops and medicines. According to the U.S. National Academy of Sciences, a typical four-square-mile patch of Amazonian rainforest contains 1,500 species of flowering plant, 125 species of mammal, 400 of bird, 100 of reptile, 60 of amphibian, 150 of butterfly, and tens of thousands of insect.

Only a tiny percentage of Amazonia's millions of species of plants and animals are known to science, but those few that have been studied have already yielded valuable foods, medicines, and commercial products. It is no exaggeration to say that without quinine and rubber, both natives of the Amazon rainforest, the histories of medicine, exploration, and industry—and of mankind—would be different. Sales of rainforest-derived medicines, including quinine and d-turbocurarine (an important anesthetic derived from the arrow poison, which Colombian Indians prepare from the bark of certain rainforest vines) amount to billions of dollars annually. The financial worth of crop improvements made by crossbreeding modern crops with their wild rainforest relatives to achieve pest resistance, higher food value, or faster growth is almost incalculable. As an example, however, the International Crops Research Institute estimates that one such interbreeding program in which cultivated peanuts were crossed with wild Amazonian peanuts to create a disease-resistant strain is worth $500 million a year to peanut farmers.

Loren McIntyre's tales of Amazonia are fascinating and instructive, and they have another laudable feature. To McIntyre, the forest is never a jungle. The word *jungle* has an overburden of mystery and danger. It also implies a challenge: conquer this wild place or be conquered. It is true that the rainforest is not a hospitable place for humans.

Amazonia, like most rainforests, is sparsely populated, and for good reason. Humans do well to respect the forest and those few who have learned to live there. Unfortunately, many people have macho attitudes toward the rainforest. As far back as 1940 this attitude was celebrated by Getulio Vargas, the then-president of Brazil, who said, "To see Amazonia is the heart's desire of the youth of this country. To conquer the land, tame the waters, and subjugate the jungle, these have been our tasks. And in this centuries-old battle, we have won victory upon victory.".

To many people, rainforests are jungles, physically and psychologically threatening until tamed. But millions more are inspired by the variety, complexity, and purposefulness of the rainforest and by the power and diversity of life there itself. For those millions, rainforests are important not only for their undoubted financial and ecological value, but also for the spiritual riches they provide us. This deep, perhaps primeval, attachment to forests that most of us know only through stories, books, and television could—if it inspires us to action—be one of the Amazon's great strengths.

The Editors
Sierra Club Books

TRINIDAD

VENEZUELA

PANAMA

COLOMBIA

*Orinoco*

Roraima
9,094

Gı

Bogotá

*Great
Cataracts of
the Orinoco*

*Orinoco*

Boa Vista

*Parima Range*

*Vaupés*

*Devils
Cataract*

San
Carlos

*Guainía*

*Branco*

TRANS-ANDEAN PIPELINE

Tiobarba
Acaricuara

*Uaupes*

*Rio Negro*

BR-174

Equator

*Coca*

Quito

Cotopaxi
19,347

P. de Orellana

*Japurá*

*Archipielago
das Anavilhanas*

Mana

ECUADOR

Sangay
17,159

*Napo*

*Putumayo*

**Amazon**

*Juruá*

*Tefé*

**Amazon**

Iquitos

Leticia

Nauta

Pongo de Manseriche

*Marañón*

*Yavari*
*Javari*

*Juruá*

*Coari*

*Purús*

*Madeira*

*Ucayali*

*Juruá*

*Purús*

BR-406

*Marañón Gorge*

**BRA**

A

Pucallpa

*Marañón*

*Huallaga*

Pôrto Velho

*Roosevelt River*

Tingo
Maria

RONDÔNIA

**PERU**

C. Esperanza

Guajará-Mirím

BR-429

BR-364

Cerros Puypuy

*Lago
de Junín*

Montalo Chico

*Madre de Dios*

*Mamoré*

Principe da Beira

*Apurímac*

*Urubamba*

*Beni*

*Guaporé*
*Iténez*

Lima

Queros

Colquepunku

*Mamoré*

Apurímac
Gorge

Cuzco

Trinidad

N

Cailloma
Mismi
18,383
(Amazon source)

Illampu
20,873

D

*Lago
Titicaca*

La Paz

**BOLIVIA**

*Colca*

Arequipa

Illimani
21,201

Cochabamba

S

CHILE

PARAGU

*Pacific*

O
c
e
a
n

Tributaries of
the Amazon

Rainforest

National boundary

Mountain peak

Major highways

# AMAZONIA

*Atlantic*

Devil's I.

SURINAME

FRENCH
GUIANA

..NA HIGHLANDS

*Trombetas*

Macapá

*Jari*

Monte Dourado

*Amazon*

Óbidos

Marajó I.

*Pará*

**Belém**

Santarém

*Tapajós*

Altamira

*Tocantins*

BR-010

Guiana Current

Equator

*Ocean*

..HIGHWAY

*Xingú*

I      L

Cachimbo

BR-080

*Araguaia*

von Martius Falls

*Bananal I.*

Xingú
National
Park

*Rio das Mortes*

..ZILIAN
HLANDS

Cuiabá

**Brasília**

Boundary of Amazonia

The brim of the
**Amazon Basin**
is the continental
divide of the surround-
ing heights—mainly the
Andes and the Guiana and
Brazilian Highlands. Northern
reaches of rainforest extend
beyond the watershed.

0                              300 miles

0                              500 kilometers

# INTRODUCTION

## REALM OF THE RAINBOW RIVERS

AMAZONIA SEEN FROM SPACE IS GREEN. A closer look reveals rainbow hues in water, leaf, and wing. This book divides Amazonia into the dominant colors—white, black, blue, and brown—of the vast river system defining its limits. The assigned colors are neither exact nor invariable, but they furnish a way of sorting out the confusion of mountains and plains, forests and savannas, tributaries and mainstream, and the creatures—including humans—that live in the basin of the rivers Amazon.

The region is almost large enough—nearly 2.5 million square miles—to cover the face of the full moon. Roughly a thousand rivers are named on detailed maps, although in truth the Amazon's tributaries are countless. Some of the smaller ones are hidden beneath the trees; others appear only when it rains.

*White water* falls from the western skies in the form of snow and rain. It gathers along Andean slopes at the lofty outer rim of the Amazon Basin and spills into rivulets and waterfalls that gradually lose their transparency as they accumulate sediment scoured from mountainsides.

*Black water* flows mainly from the north, where the Rio Negro and its warm tributaries are darkened by vegetation steeping like tea leaves forgotten in a kettle. When examined by the glassful, black water tends to resemble sherry. There are black-water lakes and swamps scattered throughout Amazonia.

*Blue water* from the south is clarified by filtering through the white crystalline sand of the central Brazilian highlands, and by the slowing of its currents and the consequent settling of sediment upon reaching large terminal lakes. Sometimes blue water turns green with algae, or gray under heavy overcast, then blue again, reflecting cloudless skies. Although some streams from the north are also blue, a group of large right-bank tributaries comprises the blue-water domain.

The *brown water* of the Amazon mainstream is colored by suspended sediment washed from crumbling lowland riverbanks and eroded from Andean rock thousands of miles upstream. Brown is the color of all the major tributaries flowing from Ecua-

convert the heathen, the pope drew a line through the Atlantic Ocean from pole to pole and assigned everything beyond it to Spain, everything short of it to Portugal. Even though he was a Borgia and the most conspiratorial of popes, Alexander VI could never have imagined the far-reaching consequences of his decision. As it turned out, an adjustment of the demarcation line gave not only Africa but also the eastern bulge of South America to Portugal. The arbitrary stroke of a Borgia pen destined half the population of South America to speak Portuguese today, half to speak Spanish, except in the Guianas, and almost all to be Roman Catholic.

The newcomers to Amazonia resolved themselves into nations in the 1820s. Most of Amazonia remained in Brazil and covers half the country. Since the watershed of the Andes bisects Bolivia, Peru, and Ecuador, half of each of those countries is Amazonian. The basin also includes about a fourth of Colombia and a fifth of Venezuela. Although their Amazonian regions are still thinly populated, all six nations are fiercely possessive about the region. Territory has changed hands dozens of times.

In Brazil's Amazonia, about 5 percent of the original vegetation was humid savanna, 12 percent was scrub, and 83 percent was tropical forest. Between 1960 and 1990 about 10 percent of the scrub and 7 percent of the forest were cleared. "Nine-tenths of the rainforest is still uncut," according to Dr. Philip Fearnside of Brazil's Amazon Research Institute. His life's work has been to keep track of increasing deforestation.

Dr. Fearnside works in Manaus, capital of the Alaska-sized state of Amazonas. "In this state only one and two-tenths of one percent, twelve acres in every thousand, are deforested, mostly around this city," he told me early in 1991. "But in the states of Rondônia and Mato Grosso, almost 15 percent of the forests have vanished in recent years, and the destruction is worsening, though not as fast as in the 1980s. It's partly because of rampant inflation. Money becomes worthless so fast that Brazilians want to invest in land and speculate with once-forested holdings."

Dr. Fearnside's computer printouts gained a third dimension when I flew around Amazonia in a small plane. In Amazonas state and across the border in southeastern Colombia, splendid forests stretched unbroken to the horizon. There was little sign of humanity. I tried to think of the region as a regulator of climate, as a key segment of global ecology, but the scenery was too dramatic to permit an exercise in intellect; it appealed to atavistic emotions. I saw a vast natural laboratory, a single organism embracing countless species, inviting all the world's seekers of knowledge to come and learn. The canopy awaits us; its upper tier, where most of its life goes on, has barely been visited. There spread the theatrical scenes I wanted to preserve in the pages of this book, so that readers might recognize the beauty as well as the environmental and economic value of Amazonia.

Dr. Fearnside's impersonal statistics for Rondônia and Mato Grosso were not nearly as disheartening as the sight from the air of the man-made scars upon the land in those states. I wondered if Kentucky had looked like this while its sycamore, hickory, and oak burned, and its bison, bears, and turkeys were being shot by Daniel Boone's settlers.

In Peru, the sight of once-forested hillsides covered with coca plantations reminded me that Amazonia produces all sorts of pharmaceuticals. The enormity of the altered landscape also made me sick.

During hundreds of hours of flying low over the canopy in the past 30 years I have seldom been able to see my best friends in the forests, the Indians of nearly three dozen tribes whom I have known but never understood as well as I wished. Indians are now far fewer than when botanist Karl Friedrich Philipp von Martius traveled among them in 1818–1820 and made an observation that still holds true:

The present and future condition of this race of men is a monstrous and tragical drama, such as no fiction of the poet ever yet presented. A whole race of men is wasting away; no power of philosophy or Christianity can arrest its proudly gloomy progress towards a certain and utter destruction. From its ruins there arises, in the most motley combination, a new and reckless generation, anxious to estrange their newly acquired country from its former masters. The east brings blood and blessings; social union and order; industry, science, and religion; but with selfish views, only for itself; for itself it erects a new world; while the race of men, which was once here the master, is fleeting away like a phantom.

I remember taking pictures of an Indian camped on a sandbar with two teen-age wives. We had become friends while he recovered from the bite of a deadly fer-de-lance; his foot was still a mess. He wanted the pictures *mailed* to him! How? Emptying his basket of manioc bread, armadillo roasted in its shell, and a Dick Tracy comic book, he took out a calling card, which I still treasure 29 years later:

WASHINGTON BOLIVAR
Jefe de la Tribu de los Cashivos
Aguaytia—Via Chambillo.

And I remember a night among the Urueu-Wau-Wau who lived in the highland center of Rondônia, where rivulets flow outward to all points of the compass before curving into the brown Madeira. The tribe still held vast territory but was surrounded by distant enemies who were closing in relentlessly. Rubber tappers, traditionally their most dangerous foes, had become environmental heroes. Lumbermen were cutting down their trees for shipment to Japan. Tin miners were despoiling their earth and betraying their children's innocence. But in the evening the settlers' chain saws ceased to snarl beyond the star-touched hills and I listened to the breathing of a warrior-to-be about six years old, Kwambr, asleep in a nearby hammock. I saw by firelight that he clutched in one hand a child-sized bow and arrow. He truly embodied the concept of endangered species. Kwambr had little chance of growing to manhood and no chance whatever of survival if he followed his father's teachings and let fly arrows at intruders.

I still listen for his breathing.

# PART I
# THE WHITE-WATER DOMAIN

# PART I

# THE WHITE-WATER DOMAIN

## THE GILDED MAN

DURING MY PICTURE-TAKING travels in upper Amazonia I often watch clouds sail westward with the prevailing winds, run aground on high mountainsides, and spill their cargo down the slopes. The distilled water cascades valleyward, aerating in ever greater leaps, until lost to sight in the thickening forest. The uppermost freshets are usually nameless, but when enough of them gather to form a river, somebody names it for a circumstance or a saint, and it becomes one of the white-water tributaries to appear on Amazonian maps.

Gravity draws down the lifeblood of Amazonia from sources as countless as capillaries. The loftiest headwaters of the venous system are found in the snowpeaked cordillera of the Andes curving through Colombia, Ecuador, Peru, and Bolivia. Lying across the equator, the range is a three-mile-high rain barrier, the westernmost rim of the catch basin that forms the Amazon. Some water vapor is driven up the slopes so high it freezes into snow and glacial ice. Old ice under glaciers holds clues—gases, spores, and dust—to the climate of upper Amazonia as far back as Inca times. When it melts, the ancient water mingles with recent rainfall in a precipitous return to the sea, where some of it may again be vaporized by the sun.

Treeless vistas at the sources of many white-water tributaries belie popular perceptions of Amazonia as a vast green sea of vegetation—or the smoldering remains of one. The cloud forest rises to about 10,000 feet. Man-made terraces step beyond it to flatten mountainsides for growing crops at altitudes as high as 13,000 feet, above 99 percent of all living matter on Earth. The terraces were built long before the Europeans arrived and very long before some people began to blame others for altering the landscape.

Almost everyone who has ever reached the Amazon's higher headwaters has gotten there not by going up the white-water tributaries from the mainstream, but by ascending the *western* slope of the Andes, crossing the Continental Divide, and descending the eastern watershed. Since prehistoric times, millions of people have made the trip, some on their mothers' backs, others, more recently, on wheels. But getting there was seldom easy, even for those who dwelt near lofty mountain passes.

The earliest accounts of travel from the Andes into Amazonia came from the Incas. Whenever the citizen-soldiers left their highland villages and farms to march down into humid forests and impose their culture on befeathered tribesmen, they came to grief. Soldier-historian Pedro de Cieza de León reported that after one frightful mix-up with a headshrinker tribe, the emperor Tupa Inca "came out fleeing, for it is bad country, that of the jungle." Down in that shadowy world of disease and poison-tipped blowgun darts, the highland Indians found no open fields where they could advance in battle array and hurl their slingstones. Warriors had to squeeze through wet undergrowth in single file, heads bent low, feet lifted high, nervously watching for snakes and for naked bowmen who might send long arrows flitting at them through the trees. Their quilted armor was unbearable in the heat. Inca sweat ran in rivulets through red war paint and swollen insect bites. By the second moon of a campaign, tunics began to rot in the warm rain.

The "green hell" tradition of Amazon travel began with Gonzalo Pizarro's search for El Dorado, the first large European expedition into headwater country. Gonzalo had gone along on his older brother Francisco's fabulous discovery and conquest of the Inca Empire. In 1533 he witnessed the melting down of 24 tons of exquisite artifacts: ransom exacted from the captured Inca Atahuallpa. After each soldier was rewarded with 45 pounds of gold and 90 of silver, Gonzalo rode with Francisco nearly 1,000 miles through the Andes to participate in the sacking of Cuzco, the gold-bedecked capital of the Inca Empire. Gonzalo ached to discover some golden cities for himself. His chance came years later, after Francisco named him governor of Quito, an Inca city high on the slope of a smoldering volcano and now capital of modern Ecuador. Gonzalo soon got wind of El Dorado, the Gilded Man, a chieftain who was said to be anointed and dusted with gold, then rafted out onto a lake, where he bathed and let the glittering ritual rain sink to the bottom.

Although the original rumor had apparently drifted down from a meteor crater lake up north in Colombia, Gonzalo impetuously decided to explore lowlands to the east, the so-called Land of Cinnamon. The avid search for cinnamon, pepper, clove, nutmeg, and mace to pep up food and drink was still the main engine that drove European overseas expeditions. At the equator, where Gonzalo stood, easterly winds pressed dark layers of nimbus clouds against snowcapped volcanoes most of the year. The weather was far wetter than it was in either western Spain or central Peru, the terrains that Gonzalo knew best.

With an army of 150 mounted Spaniards and 190 foot soldiers, 4,000 Indians carrying supplies, and thousands of pack llamas, fighting dogs, and hogs, Gonzalo plunged down into some of the densest vegetation on Earth in February 1541. It rained incessantly. His forces took 300 days to bushwhack only 100 miles through forests and swamps. Swarms of wasps and stinging gnats almost drove them all back uphill. Many of the Europeans and highland Indians were soon overcome by heat and hunger. The famished Spaniards—among the first bearers of firearms to learn that game is scarce throughout much of Amazonia—were reduced by Christmas to eating dogs and precious horses. Everyone fed on "herbs and roots and wild fruits, frogs, and serpents," and there were hints of cannibalism. Some found bitter manioc roots in Indian canoes and ate them raw. Since they lacked the forest Indians' knowledge of the need to rinse the sap out of roots, they died in agony from prussic acid poisoning.

When they reached the Río Coca, they built a small galley with wet wood and horseshoe nails. Gonzalo Pizarro sent it downriver to search for food. His foragers took along most of the arquebuses and crossbows. They never came back.

After eighteen months of floundering in thicket and quagmire under the forest canopy and struggling back up volcanic cliffs, the bedraggled conquistador reappeared in Quito. No one said, "What a fool you are," for everyone believed that hidden somewhere in the vast forests to the east there must be at least one more shining city like Cuzco that a luckier conquistador might sack.

Rumor was already transforming El Dorado from the Gilded Man to a mythical land, a vision of battlements towering above a golden kingdom on the shore of a silvery lake. During centuries to come, hordes of Spaniards and Indian bearers set forth to search for it in the headwaters regions, only to discover little more than mental anguish and physical misery. Overcome by organisms better able than they to withstand extremes of heat and humidity, many perished. Neither their exertions nor the return of their flesh to earth brought about any change perceivable today in the biomass of the cloud forest. In time, El Dorado came to signify not only a far country resplendent and unattainable, but also a mystical goal just beyond reach.

Into the twentieth century, dreamers went on fantasizing that arcadian survivors of an ancient civilization might yet dwell in upper Amazonia, but in 1911 the last wispy hope for recovering a living time capsule fell into ruins when Hiram Bingham announced his discovery of "the lost city of the Incas," an abandoned citadel towering 1,400 feet above swift headwaters in Peru. It was much closer to Cuzco than to the Land of Cinnamon, and had he learned of its existence, Gonzalo Pizarro might have found its inhabitants still there in the 1540s. Bingham's diggings revealed that the last of them died around the time of the Conquest. He found little gold in Machu Picchu, but through tourism the jungle-cloaked aerie has come to be worth far more than Atahuallpa's ransom.

I believe the Gilded Man will keep on casting his spell over the white-water domain until some distant day when energy needs have diminished the enchantment by obliging the major Andean waterfalls to descend through penstocks and turbines. Then visionaries can stay at home and compel electronic imagery to summon a hummingbird from the Land of Cinnamon to hover near the cheek of a loved one. As yet, so many ancient ruins lie hidden in the rank growth on the eastern slope of the Andes that hardly a year goes by without the discovery or rediscovery of another complex.

Another incentive to explore Amazon headwaters was to convert heathen aborigines to Christianity. To coax hunter-gatherers out of the woods and teach them to become churchgoing servants and farmers, holy men armed with rosaries carried the cross from the Andean heights down many headwaters, founding missions along the way. Hundreds of zealous Spanish priests who sought to spread the faith may have attained El Dorado if only in the hereafter, "slain by savages," their wooden churches put to the torch. According to weighty Jesuit annals that list the martyred fathers and their vanished settlements, their executioners were often members of their own flocks. Today's

The lofty rim of the basin that captures the Amazon's most distant headwaters rises 4,000 riverine miles from the mouth. The three-mile-high Continental Divide *(above)* is surprisingly free of snow and ice in this first picture ever taken from the Mismi Massif, October 15, 1971. Meltwater trickling to the left into the two-mile-deep Colca River gorge plunges 100 miles to the Pacific Ocean in a day. Drainage flowing to the right may reach the Atlantic Ocean in two months if it does not evaporate en route. ¶ Discovery of a golden idol entombed near the 18,383-foot summit of the Mismi Massif *(right)* revealed that unknown Incas left offerings on these heights 500 years ago. Beneath the northern face of the massif, the little round lake (at 15°31′s, 71°41′40″w) holds the ultimate source waters of the greatest river on Earth. In 1972, the tarn was named Laguna McIntyre by the Interamerican Geodetic Survey field authority on nomenclature of Peruvian maps.

PRECEDING PAGES: A stealthy presence, here veiled in green, this powerful cat prowls nearly all the uncivilized terrain remaining in the New World. It goes by many names: cougar, catamount, panther, puma, mountain lion, *suçuarana,* and—in Amazonia—*onça parda.* Yet all belong to a single species, *Felis concolor.*

The Qoyllur Riti (Star of the Snow) ceremony draws pilgrims of Inca heritage to the glacial source *(upper left)* of the Río Tinquimayo, an Amazon tributary. Some stay the night to sense the Earth "coming alive" under the seven-starred Pleiades, signaling the time to sow. At daybreak, devotees bring down ice from Apu Colquepunku, the god-mountain, melt it, and thicken the holy water with barley to make *api*, a rejuvenating beverage. ¶ Llamas *(above)*, domesticated in the distant past by proto-Indians, live at the upper edge of the white-water domain in symbiosis with humankind; there are no wild llamas. Toward sundown, a highland Indian woman drives her llamas past Sacsahuaman *(lower left)*, the enormous Inca fortress overlooking Cuzco, a city at the headwaters of an Amazon tributary.

Flanked by palace walls, Hatunrumiyoc (Megalith) Street *(above)* led east from the center of Cuzco toward upper Amazonia, termed Antisuyu by the Incas. Mispronouncing it Andes, Spaniards applied the Inca name of the eastern slopes to all of the 5,000-mile-long range. ¶ Among Inca descendents who still follow ancient customs and speak the imperial language are inhabitants of Queros *(right)*. Their stone village clings to a mountainside above the timberline 100 trail miles northeast of Cuzco. The rising sun warms the village; by noon, dank clouds from Amazonia envelop it; at 3:00 P.M. the sun sinks behind the mountain.

Bisecting the lost empire of the Incas west of Cuzco, the mile-deep Apurimac River gorge funnels headwaters from Mount Mismi and other sources toward the Amazon mainstream. The Apurimac's waters plummet 13,600 feet in 310 miles. When the Incas began to overrun Peru in the 1440s, their engineers spanned the Apurimac with a fiber suspension bridge for transporting armies and pack llamas. A cliffside temple by the bridge housed Apu Rimac, the Lord Oracle, said to have foretold the coming of bearded men who would subvert the Inca Empire. The oracle's effigy was a tree trunk the size of a human body, splashed with sacrificial blood. Father Cobo wrote that it had "a golden belt one palm wide, with two women's breasts of solid gold. The oracle's guardian, a hag of royal blood, kept to the shadows while incanting prophecies." When the conquering Spaniards did come riding, in 1533, "the witch threw herself from the cliff, calling on her god, Apu Rimac." ¶ For centuries no one imagined that the Apurimac was the Amazon's most distant tributary. Many a wrong source was put on a map by an adventurer, a priest, or a geographer who wished to claim for himself or his country the origin of the river long recognized as the world's greatest. As late as the 1940s the most widely accepted source was Laguna Lauricocha below Peru's Cordillera Huayhuash—whereas the true source at the Apurimac headwaters is almost 400 miles farther upstream from the Atlantic. ¶ Man's shaping of Earth's surface may relocate the Amazon source. A six-nation project diverting Apurimac headwaters through a tunnel under the Continental Divide will irrigate the Peruvian coastal desert. Then the title of "farthest tributary" may pass to the Río Mantaro, which drains 100-square-mile Lago de Junín in Peru's central highlands. The most distant freshet renewing Junín seeps from three glacial lakes at 16,700 feet, under the summits of twin snowcapped peaks named Cerros Puypuy. In time, the three lakes, Lagunas Suero Cocha, may replace Laguna McIntyre on maps showing the ultimate Amazon source.

FOLLOWING PAGES: The Río Urubamba loops around the base of Machu Picchu, lost city of the Incas, underscoring its peninsularity.

In the forest the cries that greet the dawn hush when the sun appears, as if the steamy shafts of light that pierce the canopy are batons directing diminuendo. Hidden in high foliage, an emerald tree boa *(Coralus caninus; lower left)*, has secured its prehensile tail around a branch, ready to spring from cover and throttle an unsuspecting bird. ¶ Among arboreal occupants that venture close to the forest floor are toucans *(upper left)* of the Ramphastidae family, often addressed as "You crazy bird!" in various languages by people who domesticate them. Toucans learn to patrol a house and yard, order people around, and sass them with dry, sharp, "we-trek, we-trek" grunts when they fail to shape up. ¶ A very costly bird, the cock-of-the-rock *(Rupicola rupicola; above)* clears spaces on the forest floor for courtship dancing. Indian trappers search for the secret little ballrooms and strew them with long twigs coated with resin, which stick to the bird's feet and inhibit flight—as well as mating.

Rain-ridden forests of the eastern Andean slopes *(above)* are as thick with undergrowth and as difficult to penetrate on foot as any tropical forests on Earth. ¶ September blossoms crown the forest *(right)* at 7,000 feet on summits west of Peru's upper Río Ucayali, a carrier of runoff from the Amazon's primary source.

PRECEDING PAGES: Every leaf is touched by mist in the cloud forest.

Forests of Amazonia still stood 99 percent intact four centuries after the Europeans arrived, since almost all travel and settlement were riverine. But when overland trails widened into vehicular roads during the twentieth century—as in central Ecuador *(above)*—trees began to fall. ¶ The very tears of the trees themselves hastened their fate, for until World War II the manufacture of nearly all automobile tires began by slashing the bark of *Hevea brasiliensis*. Even today the industrial name for natural rubber *(lower left)* is *caoutchouc,* an Indian term for "weeping wood." ¶ The coca leaf, source of a natural stimulant and painkiller harvested in Amazonia since ancient times, became an Inca monopoly and later the main crop of viceregal Peru. Today, worldwide consumption of cocaine is so great that coca plantations *(upper left)* are the leading reason for deforestation in the white-water domain.

The canopy of a white-water forest may be the most exuberant yet least explored level of its biome. Many of its flowers unfold from epiphytes, air-breathing plants that perch on tree limbs *(left)* beyond the easy reach of scientists. ¶ Some of the tree-dwellers are native American plants called bromeliads, members of the pineapple family. Anchored by aerial roots, many bromeliads collect water in tanklike rosettes *(above)* that harbor all sorts of small creatures from frogs to anopheles mosquito larvae. In turn, night-feeding female anopheles mosquitoes may host protozoan parasites that cause malaria, the most widespread of all deadly infectious diseases. Malaria has been treated with quinine ever since conquerors brought the disease from the Old World. Quinine is derived from the bark of cinchona trees native to this same forest.

Inside La Cueva de las Lechuzas *(left)* near Tingo María, Peru, it is wise to breathe through a wet rag to filter dust that transmits psittacosis. The ground squirms underfoot with enormous insects and grubs crawling amid husks of forest fruits and bodies of blind rats. Stalagmites pierce a floor of hardened bat guano. A flashlight beam provokes screeches hoarse and hideous enough to startle an aging troglodyte. The protesters are not owls *(lechuzas)*, but guacharos *(Steatornis caripensis)*, oil birds such as Alexander von Humboldt found in a cave he explored near Caripe, Venezuela, in 1799. He missed their nocturnal performance. ¶ At nightfall, a clicking as of distant castanets begins far inside the cave. One after another, the chicken-size birds fly from hidden perches where they nest in darkness all year round. Each click is an echo-location signal the guacharo emits to navigate amidst a maze of stalactites and a commotion of other birds. As the roiling flock nears the cavern vestibule, the clicking swells to a confused crescendo. Guacharos fly into the night by twos and threes, then dozens. Many will scout 20 or 30 miles to feed and bring back fruits from laurels and incense palms to fatten squabs heavier than adult birds. Others mill inside the vestibule all night long, broadcasting their ratchety din into the surrounding jungle. At daybreak, the clicking recedes into the mountain, and by sunup all is still.

There is a village clinging to the eastern wall of Peru's Cordillera Vilcabamba that almost deserves the appellation Shangri-La, although its name is really Montalo Chico. Few outsiders have ever found the way to this cloud forest where all ages of the Machiguenga Indians wear ankle-length gowns called *cushmas*. The people's serene demeanor echoes that of the lamasery inhabitants in *Lost Horizon*, and they do not reveal their names or ages. The headman *(above)*, who may not be as young as he seems, is not a lama but a superb hunter; guests call him Orion.   ¶ To leave the village, visitors must cross the Río Montalo on a bridge that cannot fall down *(left)*. Tall living saplings bent from opposite banks and joined above the torrent are covered with a fiber footpath. If its lashings ever fail, the bridge can only fall *up*.

# PART II
# THE BLACK-WATER DOMAIN

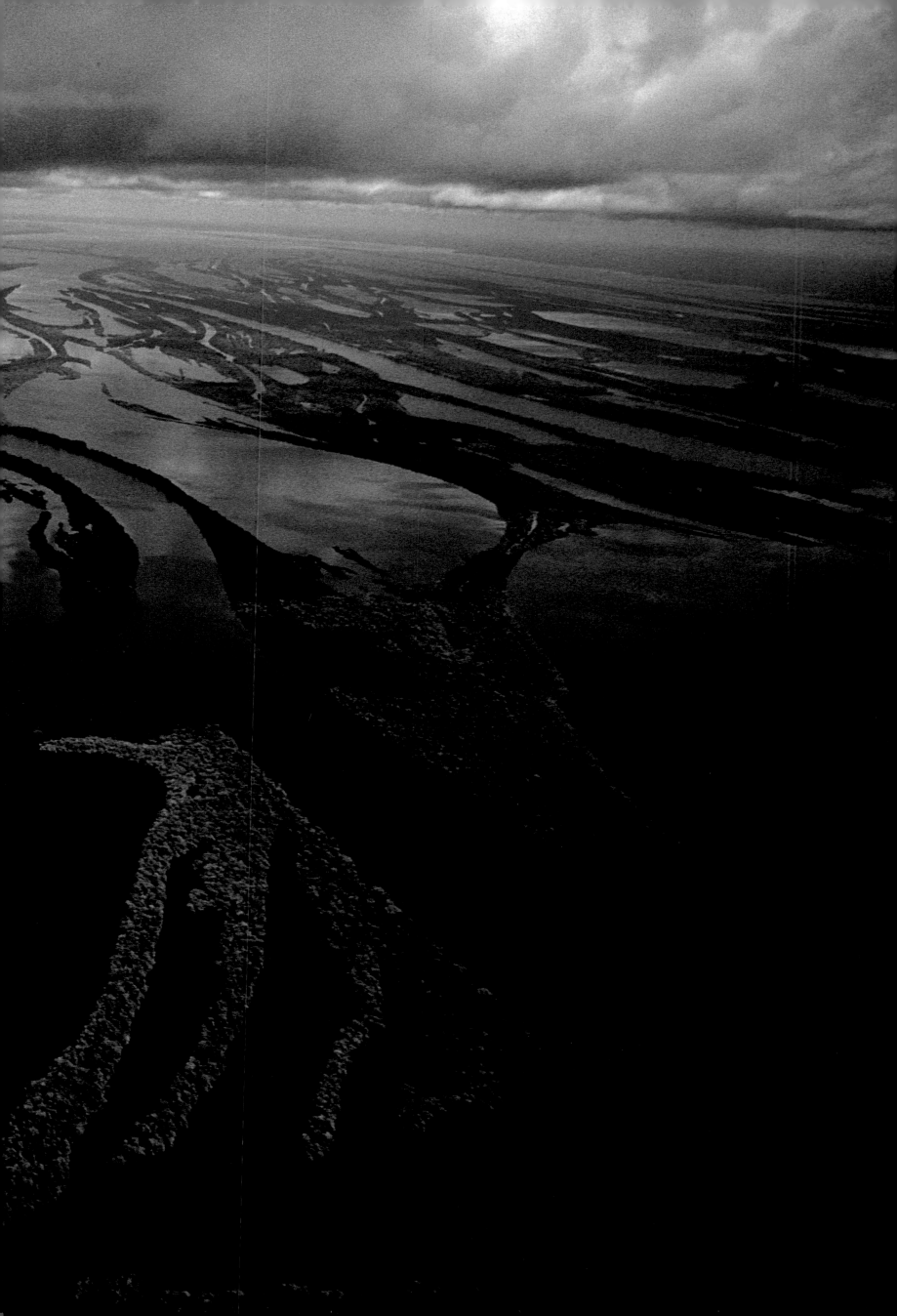

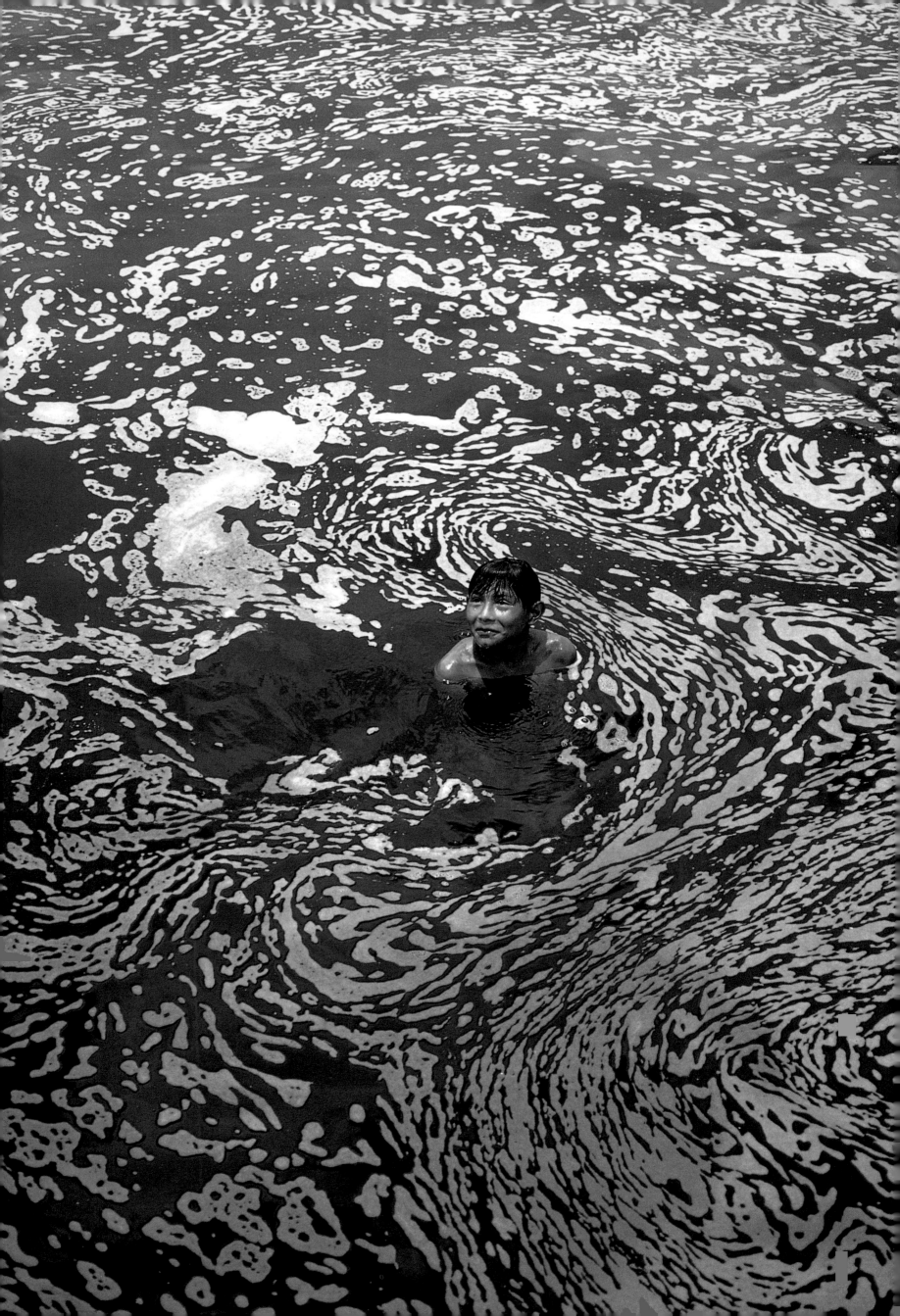

# PART II
# THE BLACK-WATER DOMAIN

## THE STYGIAN STREAM

AT THE HEIGHT of its annual flood in June, the Rio Negro nearly equals the Amazon in volume as it mixes with the mainstream in midcontinent. The stygian stream bears an enormous runoff flushed from the murky swamps and saturated forests of Colombia, Venezuela, and Brazil, which spread across the northwest quadrant of Amazonia. It is so wet a region that rivermen say, "In summer it rains every day. In winter it rains all day." Dying vegetation steeps in warm swamp water and darkens it. Concentrated runoff oozes into waterways. From the air it looks like used engine oil pouring into a pond. But aside from the stain, hardly any material is carried in suspension. Rain washes less than one pound of sediment a year from an acre of forest floor, compared to the 20,000 pounds or more that might be eroded from an acre of denuded land. Unlike the aerated freshets that leap from white-water highlands, the black-water sources are low on dissolved oxygen and high on the humic acid that discourages mosquitoes.

The Rio Negro's source waters gather at an almost imperceptible Continental Divide only 500 feet above sea level, in the Venezuelan state of Amazonas. The Divide is a vast flatland, studded with black granite domes that rise thousands of feet above the green and liquid landscape.

Some of the flatland's runoff flows north into the Orinoco, a Mississippi-sized river that curves through Venezuela like a fishhook, its point stuck in the legendary Parima Range that shapes the border with Brazil. Other runoff meanders to the south toward the Rio Negro and the Amazon. Either way, the gatherings of raindrops run more than a thousand miles, dropping only three inches every mile, until they reach the Atlantic Ocean.

It is extraordinary that both rivers, the Orinoco and the Rio Negro–Amazon, spring from the same source in the Parima Range. As a single stream named Orinoco, they cascade westward together until the current slows upon reaching the vague Divide. Then, one-third of the Orinoco's flow forks to the left under a new name, Casiquiare.

Two hundred meandering miles later the Casiquiare joins the Rio Guainía out of Colombia to become the Rio Negro.

For centuries European cartographers drew mountains in place of the Casiquiare, asserting that nowhere on Earth could two major river systems be connected by a natural waterway. To prove them wrong, Prussian naturalist Alexander von Humboldt canoed up the Orinoco in March 1800, on what turned out to be the first of the nineteenth century's famous voyages of discovery. His 40-foot dugout, a tree trunk hollowed by hatchet and fire, was manned by nine Indian paddlers, a priest, and a Frenchman—the botanist Aimé Bonpland.

"Beyond the Great Cataracts of the Orinoco an unknown land begins," wrote Humboldt, "the classical soil of fable and fairy visions . . . nations with one eye in the forehead, the head of a dog, or the mouth below the stomach." The Indians said that the stars were reflections of silver stones in Lago Parima, a mythical lake that lay between the Amazon and the Orinoco. On its shore stood a golden city, the Villa Imperial de Manoa, ruled by El Dorado, the Gilded Man. The El Dorado legend that lured pursuers across the Andes had spread like a fatal affliction all the way to the mouth of the Orinoco, where, two centuries earlier, Sir Walter Raleigh had taken up the chase that led to his beheading.

On his upriver voyage Humboldt left the Orinoco and portaged the huge canoe ten miles across the swampy Continental Divide to the Rio Negro. In contrast to the murky Orinoco, polluted with putrescent flesh of caiman and manatee, the Rio Negro was sweet and clean. Fresh-water dolphins (botos) swam like mascot whales alongside the canoe, startling the voyagers by unexpectedly snorting through the blowholes in their heads.

The Portuguese commander at São Carlos do Rio Negro discouraged Humboldt from proceeding farther downstream—a good thing, since suspicious authorities had ordered the arrest of the nosey Prussian baron, who hurried to "collect all manner of information about lands which were not his own and even about the stars overhead."

From São Carlos, Humboldt steered eastward into the lost world of the Casiquiare, where Indians called meteors "urine of the stars" and the morning dew "spittle of the stars." One night at Culimacari, a solitary granite outcrop at the water's edge, he unboxed his sextant and shot a sight of Alpha Crucis, to him "the beautiful star at the foot of the Southern Cross." He worked out the sight to fix for the first time ever the latitude of the Casiquiare confluence.

Humboldt's 200-mile struggle up the bug-ridden Casiquiare against its Amazon-bound current was the most miserable week of his five years in the Americas. It seemed as if swarms of famished mosquitoes and gnats had lain in wait for him for years and different species attacked at different hours of the day and night. He wrote in his diary of vain attempts to thwart their voracious appetites by daubing himself with rancid crocodile grease. He sketched an idea for a linen jump suit ballooned with whalebone to keep eager proboscises away from the wearer's skin.

The canoe held great batches of pressed plants, fourteen birds, eleven mammals, a crew of nine, and three Europeans—far too many to sleep decently on board. Yet there were no beaches on which to set up camp; thick gallery forests infested with wasps overhung the banks. The crew had nothing left to eat but raw cacao beans. A jaguar carried off their pet mastiff. At the end of the upstream ordeal, they regained the Orinoco at the Casiquiare bifurcation and paddled to Esmeralda, an outpost set in a meadow studded with termite hills and pineapple plants. Esmeralda's caretaker mistook them for traders when he spotted Bonpland's pile of paper for drying plants. He advised them the paper would be hard to sell since local inhabitants didn't write much.

Half a century later, while Humboldt was reigning as Europe's grand old man of science and exhausting his large inheritance by publishing magnificent volumes, a gangling Englishman in his twenties was working his way up the Rio Negro by selling insect specimens to British collectors at a few pennies each. Fascinated by the forms and behavior of creatures in the wild, Alfred Russel Wallace began to wonder whether the characteristics of species might change in response to environmental needs. Eventually, Wallace hit on the notion of "survival of the fittest" and became, with Charles Darwin, the coauthor of the theory of evolution.

Wallace's colleague at the outset of his New World travels was another amateur naturalist, Henry Walter Bates, who was destined to become the most famous of entomologists. More than 8,000 of the 14,712 species Bates collected during eleven years in Brazil were new to science. He was the discoverer of protective mimicry. A bit of an oddball, with a pin cushion and six sizes of pins fastened to his shirt, Bates walked in the forest about five hours a day.

"Over my left shoulder slings my double-barrelled gun. In my right hand I take my net; on my left side is suspended a leather bag with two pockets, one for my insect box, the other for powder and two sorts of shot; on my right hand hangs my 'game bag,' an ornamental affair, with red leather trappings and thongs to hang lizards, snakes, frogs, or large birds; one small pocket in this bag contains my caps, another papers for wrapping up delicate birds."

In *The Naturalist on the River Amazons* (1863), Bates described paddling along *igarapés*, waterways through forests flooded several months each year. To withstand inundation, the trees differ from those in drier parts of Amazonia.

On each side were the tops of bushes and young trees . . . and the trunks of the tall trees rose at irregular intervals from the water, their crowns interlocking far over our heads and forming a thick shade. Slender air roots hung down in clusters and looping *sipós* ("rope plants," or lianas, in the Tupi Indian language) dangled from the lower branches; bunches of grasses, Tillandsiae, and ferns sat in the forks of the larger boughs, and the trunks of the trees near the water had adhering to them round dried masses of fresh-water sponges. There was no current perceptible, and the water was stained of a dark olive-brown hue, but the submerged stems could be seen through it to a great depth.

When the paddlers rested for a time, the stillness and gloom of the place became almost painful; our voices waked dull echoes as we conversed, and the noise made by fishes occasionally whipping the surface of the water was quite startling. . . . The few sounds of the birds are of that pensive or mysterious character which intensifies the feeling of solitude rather than imparts a sense of life and cheerfulness.

. . . [I]n the midst of the stillness, a sudden yell or scream will startle one; this comes from some defenseless fruit-eating animal, which is pounced upon by a tiger cat or stealthy boa constrictor. Morning and evening the howling monkeys make a most fearful and harrowing noise under which it is difficult to keep up one's buoyance of spirit.

The yellows and greens of pierid butterflies are the most kinetic colors of Amazonia. Constantly on the move, the ubiquitous pierids, called *panapaná* in the black-water domain, escort visitors through sunlit woods along muddy pathways where they lay their eggs *(above)*. In the 1850s, naturalist Henry Walter Bates watched pierids swarm in shimmering clouds three to eight miles long across the broad Rio Negro. ¶ Many species of heliconia *(right)* have been transplanted from Amazonian forests to urban tropical gardens in Brazil—particularly those pioneered by landscape architect Roberto Burle Marx.

PRECEDING PAGES: Reflections from a submerged white sandbar at the upstream end of an island in the Rio Negro show that black water turns to "wine" in the shallows.

The deadliest mammal in Amazonia is *Homo sapiens*. He kills for reasons other than hunger, and also murders his own species. Native Americans such as the Yanomamö boy *(above)* long ago learned to make weapons that may have been instrumental in eliminating from Amazonia all huge land animals except the tapir. ¶ The largest mammal native to Amazonia is the tapir *(Tapirus terrestris; upper right)* at about 500 pounds. A relative of the horse and rhinoceros, the tapir has a short, elephantine trunk. The animal is inoffensive, and tame ones have even been known to go swimming in the Amazon with people. ¶ The longest lizard in Amazonia is the jacuruxi *(Dracaena guyanensis; lower right)*, at about four feet, more than half of which is tail. Although *Dracaena* is derived from the Greek word for "she-serpent" or "dragon," the red-headed *guyanensis* lizard is inoffensive to all but the smallest mammals. The jacuruxi feeds both in the trees and in the water.

PRECEDING PAGES: Chacobo Indians in the family's dugout canoe navigate an inundated forest in northernmost Bolivia.

The Devil's Cataract, *Yuruparí,* blocks navigation on Colombia's black-water Río Vaupés *(above)* just before it enters Brazil to merge eventually with the Rio Negro. The Indian fish trap *(right)* deflects some cataract water onto a slanting platform of palm slats. When the water falls through the cracks, large fish get stranded on the slats.

At Acaricuara *(above)*, on a black-water tributary of the Vaupés, Catholic priests and nuns teach religion, literacy, and agriculture to children of the Tucano, Desano, Tujuca, Yuruti, and Siriano tribes. Many of the children's families subsist by fishing, hunting woodland creatures, and gathering fruits and nuts in the vast forests of southeastern Colombia. But when Indians come in from the wilderness to settle in "civilized" communities, they tend—or are forced—to leave their self-sufficiency behind. Much of the food at the Acaricuara mission table has been contributed by international donors.

A Yanomamö tribeswoman weaves a cotton hammock *(upper right)*. Her nation of many related tribes and many thousands of Indians is scattered among the headwaters of the Río Orinoco in Venezuela and the Rio Branco in Brazil. ¶ Paint once substituted for clothing among all Amazonian tribes *(lower right)*, and ancient customs are still in vogue along the upper Orinoco tributary of the Amazon. Some Yanomamö still grind the bones of their deceased and add them to soup. And to find a gourmet delicacy, they put an ear to a dead palm trunk and listen for the crunching of an edible grub burrowing through the pith.

Christopher Columbus carried back to Europe a *hamaca* spun of vegetable fiber, a Native American artifact now termed—along with the canoe—a "core element" of Amazonian culture. In the ensuing five centuries, no invention has surpassed the hammock as a portable device for sleeping safely above the ground. The classic hammock design of forest dwellers is preferred by a Makiritare tribeswoman of the upper Orinoco and her pet toucan *(lower left)*. ¶ A young voyager *(above)* has slung her hammock on the women's side of a riverboat. Made in Fortaleza, very wide cotton hammocks are amazingly comfortable when slept on slantwise. Travelers to Brazil's far frontiers usually include them in their baggage. ¶ A Brazilian hammock catches the wind *(upper left)*.

Fishing is easiest for egrets *(right)* in the "dry" season, after translucent black rivers have fallen far enough to leave quiet shallows where the great white herons wait for appetizers to swim within range. The birds snap up many an exotic minnow valued by tropical-fish fanciers. The egrets themselves used to be valuable. Sale of their nuptial plumes to milliners and potentates brought the snowy herons close to extinction around 1900. Then, avant-garde conservationists began to snatch *aigrettes* from ladies' hats and press governments to ban the plumes. Nowadays, at nesting time countless trees in tropical America become almost completely whitened with unmolested egrets.   ¶ In a forest pool on the Brazil–Venezuela frontier *(above)*, shallows reveal that black water is really a tea of decaying leaves. In this instance it is further reddened by the presence of jasper in underlying rocks and brushed with chameleonic shadows and highlights. Reflections catch dark green traces of overhanging plants and the ephemeral azure of clear skylight.

PRECEDING PAGES: A hollowed tree trunk is a plaything on the Río Vaupés, a Colombian tributary of Brazil's Rio Negro.

Along the waterfront around Manaus *(above)*, where property lines are blurred by the 40-foot annual rise and fall of the Rio Negro, the coolest air and best views of sunset over the river are enjoyed by citizens whose ramshackle homes stand on stilts in the yielding ground.

Manaus, the only large city in the black-water region, rises near the confluence of the Rio Negro and the mainstream in central Amazonia, 900 miles inland. While still wrapped in rainforest during the rubber boom nearly a century ago, Manaus tried to evoke remembrances of Paris with its ornate mansions, an ironwork fish market, streetcars, and a monumental opera house. Now the Teatro Amazonas *(above)* is surrounded by office buildings, while tourist shops, cruise ships, factories, and a burgeoning electronics industry lend Manaus the pale appearance of a lesser Hong Kong.

FOLLOWING PAGES: Canoe-borne squatters have nailed houses together along a forested shore of the Rio Jarí, Pará, Brazil.

# PART III
# THE BLUE-WATER DOMAIN

# PART III

# THE BLUE-WATER DOMAIN

## THE XINGÚ SANCTUARY

OF THE SEVEN great tributaries that enter the Amazon from the south, the most mysterious is the blue-water Xingú. Most of the upper Xingú region remained terra incognita until the middle of this century, and its occupants were unknown. The very sound of the name, Shin-GOO, evokes visions of secret places: Xanadu, Cipangu.

From ancient uplands in midcontinental Brazil, halfway along an imaginary 1,800-mile line connecting Rio de Janeiro with Manaus, the Xingú headwaters drain north, drawing dendritic patterns on savannas where emus gallop in imitation of ostriches. Dead-water channels link large lagoons fringed with burití palms where tapirs seldom grow to a full 500 pounds anymore because they are not wary enough of bronze men armed with bows and arrows. The Indians dwell where the branching waterways edged with gallery forests merge to form the main trunk of the Xingú. Only the Txukahamẽi lived on the riverbank beyond, where the river flows serenely north through virgin forest for 100 miles.

Just as the glassy Xingú approaches the precise geographic center of Brazil, rocks shatter the surface. Steep waves swirl every which way. Afterwards, the river flows quietly for 98 miles through encompassing forest. At low water its current is as transparent as an aquarium window, revealing turtles and stingrays on the bottom.

In its next transfiguration, the Xingú cascades through sixteen separate rapids and files narrowly between black-rock dikes and tall midstream boulders for 250 tortuous miles. At high water it roars, and riverine legends assert that whirlpools wait for years to suck unsuspecting canoeists out of sight. But long before it enters the *café-com-leite* Amazon, the Xingú widens into a 600-square-mile cerulean lake whose surface may turn green with algae or gray under overcast.

Even with so many obstacles to navigation, it seems odd that the upper Xingú remained unexplored so long. The river's mouth is only 300 river miles from Belém, the largest city in Amazonia. Since its founding in 1616, Belém has been host to foreign intrigue and local uprisings, to commerce in both river and forest extracts, and, in past centuries, to many an expedition bent on dragging Indians into mission compounds or into slavery on coastal plantations. Yet apparently, no slavers ever carried to the upper Xingú their cargoes of neck and ankle chains in both adult's and children's sizes.

In the early 1600s, *bandeirantes*, rampaging bands of frontiersmen from São Paulo in the south, ranged far inland and sometimes struck it rich in gold or gems or slaves, but only one small band ran the Xingú. In the late 1800s, *seringueiros*, collectors of natural rubber, fanned out to Brazil's farthest frontiers but left untouched the upper Xingú's scrubby forests. Even the Jesuits—suicidally zealous in their attempts from 1549 to 1773 to convert infidels accused of polygamy and cannibalism—never ventured above the big bend of the Xingú.

When explorers began to probe Xingú headwaters they all came up from Cuiabá, a town south of the Amazon watershed. They discovered that a dozen tribes speaking as many languages had taken refuge along the waterways. Karl von den Steinen, a young, well-traveled ethnographer, was the first to report having contacted them. Very excited about his find, Steinen regarded the "Xinguanos" as real people, not just as creatures wild as eagles, to be studied or, if necessary, shot at. Although events described in Steinen's delightful writings occurred in 1884, they mirror the felicity of Columbus's initial impressions of Indians in October 1492.

Other German expeditions followed Steinen's, but no accounts of their adventures and findings were published in English. The word *Xingú* did not appear in English-language newspapers until Percy H. Fawcett's disappearance in 1925. Fawcett, a retired British army colonel who understood boundary surveying, was sent to the upper Amazon in 1906 to resolve the overlapping claims of Bolivia and Peru arising from the rubber boom. Fawcett's reports mixed hard facts with full measures of fancy:

We were drifting easily along . . . when there appeared . . . a giant anaconda. I sprang for my rifle . . . and hardly waiting to aim smashed a .44 soft-nosed bullet into its spine, ten feet below the wicked head. . . . Shivers ran up and down the body like puffs of wind on a mountain tarn. . . . A length of 45 feet lay out of the water and 17 feet in it, making a total length of 62 feet. . . . A penetrating, fetid odor emanated from the snake, probably its breath, which is believed to have a stupifying effect, first attracting and later paralyzing its prey. Anacondas are . . . known to seize cattle at times and even to pick men out of canoes at night, their normal feeding time. . . . Anacondas give voice to melancholy wails by night, a weird sound I have heard scores of times.

When I tried to verify Fawcett's observations, Smithsonian herpetologists told me that the longest anacondas on record fell short of 28 feet and that only Fawcett reported wailing. At age 58, Fawcett got the North American Newspaper Alliance to support his quest for a secret city he called Z, "the lost remnants of a once mighty civilization." In 1925, he rode boldly into Xingú headwaters country with his eldest son, Jack, 22 (whom he described as being "big, very powerful physically, and absolutely virgin in mind and body"), and Jack's friend Raleigh Rimell.

Fawcett carried no radio but that didn't matter since several spiritualists, including his wife, claimed to be in contact with him. When I was a schoolboy I read in the Sunday papers that Fawcett had been ordained as a white god of the savages.

In 1928, the news syndicate sent Commander George M. Dyott to locate Colonel Fawcett. Leading a hazardous expedition in five large canvas boats from the source to the mouth of the Xingú, Dyott discovered evidence that Kalapalo tribesmen might have murdered Fawcett. When word spread through the Xingú that Dyott's people carried a rich trove of steel knives, canoes full of acquisitive warriors surrounded their camp. Every day brought more warriors armed with clubs and bows and arrows. In the nick of time the outlanders escaped downriver at night.

In Seattle, my small crystal set picked up a Dyott radio report broadcast by the Associated Spotlight Review. Little did I guess that 28 years later, in the upper Amazon, I would play the role of Jack Fawcett in a Warner Brothers film, *Manhunt in the Jungle*, based on the Fawcett and Dyott expeditions. Ten years after that I stumbled upon an English recluse in a jungle redoubt 30 miles south of the equator. It was Dyott, then 86.

During World War II, it appeared that a trailbreaking string of airstrips connecting Rio to Manaus would transgress the Indian haven in the upper Xingú region. But three brothers who had joined Brazil's "March to the West" in 1943 managed to spin a miracle out of the project and gain one more generation of asylum for the tribes. Orlando, Claudio, and Leonardo Villas Boas fell under the spell of the Xinguanos and decided to remain among them to defend their culture against all comers. I remember Orlando best as the merry extrovert who stepped down from a Brazilian Air Force DC3 shirtless, mosquito-bitten, carrying a stack of his favorite comic books under his arm. He was the fat one. The thin one was Claudio, an introvert who usually dwelt alone downriver with his nose buried in a philosophy book. Leonardo had died in 1961.

They were disciples of Cândido Mariano da Silva Rondon, a frontier-born orphan who rose to fame as a great explorer, an unyielding champion of the Indian, and the highest ranking officer in the history of the Brazilian army. He won headlines in the United States for having led former president Theodore Roosevelt on an expedition down a river whose very existence had been questioned by geographers. The Rio da Dúvida—River of Doubt—now appears on maps as the Rio Roosevelt. Rondon pioneered a telegraph line—the Indians called it "Mariano's tongue"—through virgin territory now a Brazilian state, Rondônia. His personal creed for contact with aborigines of the forest became the motto of the federal Indian agency he helped found: *Morrer, se fôr preciso; matar nunca!*: "Die if necessary; never kill!"

FUNAI, the successor of Rondon's Indian agency, administered the Villas Boas brothers' project. The Brazilian Air Force helped. Big city newspapers were pro-Villas Boas, even advocating for them the Nobel Peace Prize; not so the journals in frontier towns hardly out of range of Indian arrows.

Convinced that integrated Indians—even if they survive contact with disease, alcohol, and denaturalizing abuse—are no longer Indians but merely lesser citizens of Brazil, the brothers persuaded the government to create Xingú National Park in 1961. They worked ceaselessly to attract into the park warlike tribes that "the Xinguanos themselves had long dismissed as too wild and dangerous to be considered human," in Orlando's words. He and Claudio recognized that winning the friendship of Indians and persuading them to stop fighting one another and trespassers only opened up their lands more quickly to road builders and pioneers. But the alternative was violent extinction of the holdout tribes and their culture—along with whatever key knowledge of nature they had acquired during untold generations of living in the forest.

For 35 years, until they gradually surrendered to advancing age and countless bouts

A Kamayurá shaman animates the lodgepole of the men's house *(above)* by Laguna Ipavú of the Rio Kuluené.   ¶ Waurá warriors decorate each other *(upper right)* for the *Tauarauanã* dance ceremony in their village by the Rio Batoví.   ¶ Crushed seeds of urucú *(Bixa orellana; lower right)*, also known as achiote and annatto, provided the pigmentation for South America's traditional "red men" of the forest.

PRECEDING PAGES: Impassable rapids above the big bend of the lower Rio Xingú safeguard the headwaters from river traffic.

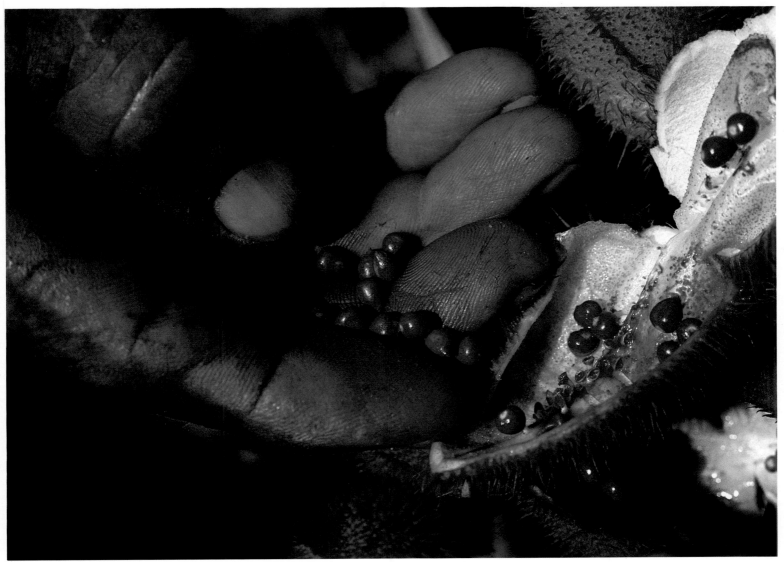

Native plants provide for most of the forest peoples' needs, from medicines to transport. Both trunk and bark stripped by a Kamayurá matron *(above)* will be used in her house by Laguna Ipavú, on the upper Xingú.   ¶ Food will be served on the mat *(right)* woven in a Karajá village by the Rio Araguaia, upper Tocantins.

Yesterday's warrior, an elderly archer *(above)*, has decorated his skin with keloids raised by burning self-inflicted wounds with caustic juices. He has fathered a dozen children who live in a Suyá village on the Rio Suiá Missu, tributary of the upper Xingú. To his people, the balsa lip disk is a thing of beauty.

Tomorrow's parents, Ipauaká and his bride, Kayanakú *(above)*, together constitute 1 percent
of the surviving members of the Tupí-speaking Kamayurá tribe. For many years their world
remained young while resident frontiersmen Orlando and Claudio Villas Boas were able to
resist most incursions of unwanted modernity into the upper Xingú region.

Two girls, two boys, two dogs, and two birds pair up in the sandy Xingú soil around a Txicão house-to-be *(above)*. The Villas Boas brothers coaxed the Carib-speaking Txicão into the Xingú reserve when attacks by Indian neighbors and the advance of armed Brazilians—hunters, prospectors, and settlers—threatened the Txicão with extinction.

Except when gathered into a mission and taught by priests and nuns to obey—as the young Xavantes *(above)* at São Marcos in Mato Grosso—Indian boys never need to fear punishment. Fathers chat with sons and teach them to fish and shoot and dance and fight and how to behave in a free society that knows neither please nor thank you nor headmen who command.

Scourge of the canopy and master of vertical flight, the harpy eagle *(Harpia harpyja; right)* flits from branch to branch like a twenty-pound hummingbird. With talons as big as a man's hand it seizes motionless sloths and fleeing monkeys. Normally, it nests in the tallest of trees, but every Xingú tribe keeps one captive in a conical cage, enthroned on a crossbar as a symbol of tribal power. ¶ Kuikuro boys romp in the rain *(above)* as free as the mightiest of eagles in the tepee behind them would like to be.

In midcontinental Mato Grosso, where, in 1914, Theodore Roosevelt explored the blue waters that laze north from ancient uplands, a Cintas Largas child plays with a deep-sea diving helmet in the Rio Aripuanã *(right)*. A witchcraft myth explains how the helmet came to be there:

> Long ago a raft came slowly upstream, moving against the current. A stranger stood upon it, not paddling, but squatting and standing, squatting and standing, see, like this! Hah! We filled the man so full of arrows he looked like a porcupine. The current carried him away but the raft stayed in place, held by a slender black snake. After a few days Macaráp, our bravest hunter, swam out to kill the snake. Hah! It was tough. No entrails. Macaráp pulled it up to chop off its head. It had a human head, nibbled by fish, and the bones of a man.

Blue waters ripple over cryptocrystalline quartz—red, brown, green, and yellow—and over sediment-free riverbeds that glisten with diamond-bearing gravel. Prospectors walk on the bottom with lead diving shoes, pulling along their support rafts with air hoses fed by hand pumps that assistants tend. The divers gather gravel by the basketful and send it up to be sorted later. Sometimes diamonds lure the bottom-walkers too far into Indian territory.

*Serrasalmus nattereri,* the most dangerous of many species of the carniverous and cannibalistic piranha *(above),* is easily attracted to the surface by a dropped speck of meat. So razor-sharp and precisely occluded are its teeth that Indian weavers use the jawbones as scissors. Piranhas seldom bother people, but experts warn that they are as unpredictable as sharks.

An archer-fisherman of the Kamayurá tribe *(above)* shoots at a stingray—as tasty as a piranha—lying motionless on the sandy bottom of Laguna Ipavú. To avoid stepping on a stingray, waders must be careful to splash a lot and shuffle their feet. A stingray's sawtooth spine tears a jagged wound that takes much longer to heal than a surgically clean piranha bite.

FOLLOWING PAGES: Munducurú Indian girls chase butterflies in the sands of the Rio Cururú, a tributary of the blue-water Tapajós in Brazil.

Climbing trees and swimming rivers, ranging forests and grasslands throughout Amazonia, the jaguar *(Panthera onça; right)* is the New World's greatest cat—weighing up to 250 pounds. Indians of both forest and highland claimed jaguar ancestry, and the animal's pelts are still worn for ritual dancing in the Andes. A 1967 law against hunting wild animals in Brazil did not stop the exportation of pelts in following years in which nearly half a million felines were killed. Since the early 1970s, outcries and international controls have granted a better chance of survival to the two or three kittens in each jaguar litter. The hunting ban is now embedded in Brazil's new constitution. ¶ Crocodilians are also protected, but not from attack by jaguars *(above)*.

The guará, or maned wolf *(Chrysocyon brachyurus; above)*, is not a wolf but a dog so tall that natives call it "fox-on-stilts." Its height enables it to see over the grass of savannas that cover vast reaches of Amazonia. Solitary, nocturnal, and nonthreatening, preying mainly on rodents, the guará is a victim of its own curiosity; it pauses to look back at pursuers, thus giving hunters a killing shot. Unable to survive captivity for long, the guará is a vanishing species.

The urubú-rei, or king vulture *(Sacroramphus papa; above)*, is called "the condor of the tropical forest," though it is smaller than the Andean bird. It once ranged as far north as the
United States, and appeared in Mayan manuscripts as the glyph for Cib, the thirteenth day of
the month. As befitting a ruler, the king vulture always dominates a carrion feast; lesser vul-
tures back off until it is finished. Its bizarre face and great flapping wings startle humans and
scare the wits out of monkeys.

Easternmost of the great Amazon tributaries, which rival all other world rivers in size, the Tocantins *(left)* winds nearly 3,000 miles from its source in the Rio das Mortes, River of the
Dead.   ¶ When the Tocantins' flow was interrupted by the world's fourth-largest dam, Tucuruí, Brazilian contractors failed to clear all of the 800 square miles of forest due for inundation. Many trees drowned *(above)*. Some are now being salvaged by divers using underwater
chain saws.

FOLLOWING PAGES: An island emerging from the drowned Tucuruí forest has become a
cramped wildlife refuge.

# PART IV
# THE BROWN-WATER DOMAIN

# PART IV

# THE BROWN-WATER DOMAIN

## THE RIVER SEA

AT 8:45 P.M. on March 5, 1987, several million trees and the earth beneath them began to shake and slide downhill and within a minute about 10,000 acres of rainforest in eastern Ecuador ceased to exist. Avalanches triggered by a Richter force 7 earthquake stripped the cover from dozens of mountain slopes and dumped the stupendous debris into affluents of the Río Napo, a major Amazon tributary.

That evening a folk music combo had been entertaining some Cuban travelers in an army post at Puerto Francisco de Orellana, a river town named after the first European to descend the river. Led by Antonio Núñez Jiménez, Cuban vice-minister of culture, they were beginning a long voyage to Havana. In four large dugout canoes manned by scientists, they planned to descend the Amazon to Manaus, paddle up the Rio Negro, cross into Venezuela through the Casiquiare, and float down the Orinoco to the Atlantic. Then they would wait until 1992, when they would sail the Caribbean from Trinidad to Cuba to celebrate Columbus's discovery of the New World in 1492.

Núñez was stamping his foot in time to the beat of a big drum when the floor stamped back and knocked him off balance. To shouts of *"Terremoto!"* everyone dashed outside. Billowing flames etched the horizon. They came from Ecuador's trans-Andean petroleum pipeline, ruptured by the first of several massive earthquakes.

"It rained all night *como loco,* like crazy," Núñez told me later. "At 11:10, a tremendous shock drove us outside again. In the morning we got under way, feeling safer on the river although we felt aftershocks right through the water and the hulls of our canoes. The river level had fallen; landslides had dammed the headwaters. Then these barriers burst one after another and walls of muddy water thickened with fallen trees swept downstream. The Napo soon became clogged with masses of fallen forest. We could have walked across the river on tree trunks, half a mile from one bank to the other, without wading, if it weren't for tangles of branches still loaded with wasps' nests and snakes. We beached our canoes."

For two days Núñez watched the vast confusion of tree trunks sweep downriver. He calculated that the raft of debris was 150 miles long. It stank of dead *bagres*—big catfish—and bloated cows with feet pointing up like the masts of macabre ships.

Twenty days after the quake, remnants of Ecuadorean forest were still floating past Leticia, Colombia, where I met Núñez at a many-countried conference on Amazonian ecology. We supposed that thousands of trees and most of the mud generated by the landslides eventually reached the Atlantic Ocean, an insignificant addition to the enormous amount of earth eroded by normal weathering.

Suspended sediment colors the Amazon brown. Imagine 30 lanes of trucks, each loaded with ten tons of silt and clay, moving bumper to bumper at three miles an hour across South America, day and night. Their speed and carrying capacity would equal that of the Amazon mainstream, which pours nearly one thousand million tons of sediment and dissolved minerals into the Atlantic Ocean every year. Nearly all the river's burden is eroded from the Andes, a mountain range composed mainly of the sedimentary floors of ancient seas crumpled upward as the heavier basaltic bottom of the Pacific Ocean rides under the continent. The mountains are still rising as fast as they are being worn down by wind, rain, ice—and earthquakes such as the one Antonio Núñez Jiménez witnessed on the Río Napo.

Núñez had been following the 1542 route of Francisco de Orellana, the first European to descend the Amazon to the sea. Orellana commanded the galley that Gonzalo Pizarro sent in search of food. Unable to return upriver and rejoin Pizarro because of the current, Orellana sailed on down the Napo and the ever-widening Amazon, leaving Pizarro to struggle back to Quito in despair and rage at the desertion of his second-in-command with 50 followers.

A priest, Friar Gaspar de Carvajal, kept an account of Orellana's eight-month voyage. Even allowing Carvajal some exaggerated accounts intended to impress the Spanish king, the riverbanks he describes seem to have been controlled by large Indian nations and to have been much more densely settled in 1542 than nowadays. At first the Indians were friendly, but after the explorers had shot and hanged a few, flotillas of archers contested Orellana's passage during the final 2,000 miles, forcing the Europeans to keep to the middle of the great river. Spanish arquebuses and crossbows saved many a day, although three Spaniards were mortally wounded by poison arrows and Friar Carvajal was injured by fierce female archers, who excelled their men in battle. They reminded him of the bellicose "Black Amazons of Californie" for whom the river was eventually named.

The Black Amazons were characters in the fantasy fiction of those times, the chivalric romances churned out by the newly invented printing press from 1490 onwards. The best-known Spanish literary superman, Amadís de Gaula, fought through thousands of battle-saturated pages, slaying hordes of infidels in imaginary lands to win honor, gold, and glory. Such fantasies, retold in ballads, almost came true for Spanish swordsmen drawn into splendidly illogical adventures by the discovery of the New World. They took enormous risks to transform themselves into hidalgos *(hijos de algo)*, "somebodies." It was no wonder that Friar Carvajal felt he was living the very pages of Book V of *Amadis*, locked in combat with the Black Amazons of Californie, when long-haired, skirted warriors darkened the sky with arrows.

Orellana got lost in the delta's skein of tidal waterways, which he later described as a *marañon*, "a maze"—one of the river's early names. When he cleared land, the swift Guiana current carried him 1,200 miles along the coast to Trinidad and reunion with compatriots.

Orellana's feat failed to secure the Amazon for Spain. For a century no one else descended the river. English, Dutch, French, and Portuguese rivals struggled for control of territory near the river's mouth, enlisting thousands of Indian warriors who relished the spectacle of tribal enemies being felled by firearms. By 1631 the Portuguese had prevailed. But, in 1637, two Spanish priests fleeing from killer Indians in Ecuador canoed all the way down the Amazon, retracing Orellana's voyage of discovery and alarming the Portuguese governor. Acting quickly to secure the hinterland for Portugal, the governor engaged one of the priests, Domingo de Brieva, to return upriver as guide into the unknown region for a fleet of 47 large canoes manned by 70 soldiers and 1,100 Indians—to this day the biggest of all Amazon expeditions. He put in charge 70-year-old Pedro Teixeira, a veteran commander of canoe flotillas during the river wars. In eight months of hard paddling Teixeira reached the headwaters of the Río Napo, staking out royal possession of lands at every encampment. By relocating 2,000 miles upriver the western boundary of territory claimed by Portugal, Teixeira's expedition gained most of the Amazon Basin for the future nation of Brazil. Yet neither Teixeira's nor Brieva's name appears on today's maps.

With part of his small army Teixeira ascended the mountainous cloud forest that had defeated Gonzalo Pizarro. Entering Quito through the back door, he surprised the Spaniards, who had ruled the city for a century. After several months the Spaniards tired of Teixeira and showed him the door. Father Brieva accompanied him back downstream—thus becoming the first and probably the only person in history to run the Amazon three times by canoe.

Brieva's sole rival on my honor roll of unsung Amazon voyagers is John Schultz, a teen-age American who set out alone from Quito in 1947 on a roundabout return to classes at the University of Chicago. With a 50-pound pack on his back and $21 in his pocket Schultz hiked over the Andes and paddled a narrow dugout canoe down the Río Napo. In Iquitos, Peru, he paid $11 for a *casco*, a seventeen-foot dugout of soft, light *cedro* widened by fire. Paddling it from the bow and covering as many as 110 miles a day, Schultz made it to Manaus, 2,000 miles downriver, on his nineteenth birthday. There friends helped him fit the dugout with sails, a centerboard, and planks to increase freeboard to eight inches. He set forth anew and stayed in midstream, where floating debris marked the correct channels; he often slept on board.

In the maze of delta estuaries where the current slackens twice a day with oceanic tides, Schultz lost his way, just as Orellana had 405 years earlier. He watched a *pororoca* tear up trees along a shallow shore and heard its awesome roar. He escaped the full force of the tidal bore since he was sailing in deep water and the tall wave—which depends on "shallow bottom effect" to give it height—flattened beneath him. He headed into the open ocean equipped with only a compass, a plastic lifeboat sextant, some navigation books as yet unread, a kerosene lamp, and a hand pump that he had to operate hourly day and night to keep his leaky canoe afloat. Contrary winds and currents held him four days in the Amazon's mouth.

Weakened by illness and near starvation, John Schultz rode the Amazon-tinted ocean current to Devil's Island, once a French prison, and on to Trinidad, where Orellana's voyage also had ended. Then he guided his dugout into Caribbean waters so transparent that they did not seem to carry in suspension even the finest sediment eroded from the Andes. Having left astern at last the final traces of the river sea, the young voyager sailed on to Miami, Florida, 6,000 miles closer to school than the upper Río Napo, where his transcendental trip had begun fourteen months earlier.

Of the brown-water tributaries loaded with sediments, the biggest is the Rio Madeira, which delivers its burden into the Amazon 90 miles downriver from Manaus. Most of the Madeira's headwaters rise in Bolivia, flowing from 21,000-foot peaks bordering Lake Titicaca, from culverts beneath La Paz, capital of Bolivia, and from brooks around lowland towns named (in translation) Conception, Exaltation, Perseverance, and Thought.

The Madeira also delivers wild rubber downriver from Bolivia to the Amazon for export to world ports—though much less, nowadays, than when the rubber boom began to peak a century ago. Before the boom began, the sap of the "weeping wood" had been used mainly for waterproofing clothing and molding such oddities as the comically indecent figurines still peddled by vendors in Amazon waterfront markets. In 1830, exports amounted to only a piddling 150 tons. By 1870, they had multiplied 40-fold. The growing demand prompted British interests to steal some *Hevea brasiliensis* seeds for growing in Asian plantations. In 1888, John B. Dunlap invented a practical rubber tire and within two decades Brazil was exporting 100 million pounds of wild rubber a year at nearly three dollars a pound. The boom furnished Manaus, a small town in the middle of Amazonia, with a floating dock, an opera house, and the first electric streetcar system in South America.

Black rock outcroppings on the upper Madeira create impassable rapids. The uppermost rubber portage was at Cachuela Esperanza near Bolivia's northern tip, where waters of the Madre de Dios, Beni, and Mamoré rivers pour turbulently into the Madeira. At that control point one of the most powerful rubber barons, Nicolás Suárez, set up warehouses and headquarters for his private army. He held 12 million acres of forest with the best wild rubber trees and employed 10,000 rubber tappers, mostly migrants from Bolivia's high Andes. Suárez was not a nice man. He murdered friends as well as enemies. He enslaved hundreds of Indians at gunpoint to carry huge balls of rubber around the ten rapids, seven cataracts, and three waterfalls that blocked steamship traffic downriver.

On a visit to Cachuela Esperanza in 1971 I found Suárez's grave. It was marked by a rusty 1909 Packard mounted on a pedestal. With only 200 yards of road to travel in front of his warehouses, the petty despot used to don his duster on Sundays and drive the Packard back and forth in style.

In the 1860s U.S. entrepreneurs attempted to build a railroad around the Madeira rapids from a downriver base near present-day Pôrto Velho to an upstream terminal at Guajará-Mirím on the Bolivian border. They were thwarted by Indian attacks, soggy terrain, and malaria—an Old World disease that spread throughout Amazonia early in the nineteenth century and is still epidemic at the close of the twentieth. A thousand workers, many from the United States, had given up their lives by 1879, when a scant four miles of track had been laid. A Baldwin locomotive made a Fourth of July run, flying both U.S. and Brazilian flags. It jumped the tracks, and soon the project expired.

The same year that the Baldwin jumped its tracks, 1879, Bolivia lost its Pacific coast in a war with Chile. That disaster accentuated its need for access to the Atlantic via the Amazon, but for 23 years rank growth enveloped the Baldwin and rubber gatherers' families used its boiler to heat bath water. Someone stole the whistle.

In 1903, for 2 million British pounds and a pledge to complete the railroad around the rapids, Bolivia ceded to Brazil 37.7 million acres of rubber-rich forest, which is now the state of Acre. From 1907 to 1912, U.S. contractors employed 21,717 men from 42 countries to build the Estrado de Ferro Madeira–Mamoré—the "Devil's Railroad," in the workers' parlance. Administrators expected to keep laborers alive by minding their health. They issued 25 tons of quinine pills to combat malaria. Even so, of 300 to 600 occupied beds in a well-staffed hospital, about one a day was vacated by death from malaria, beriberi, yellow fever, dysentery, or lethal multinational brawls, while perhaps 2,000 other workers disappeared from sight along the line. In fear of miasmic vapors thought to cause malaria, 200 Spaniards lured from the Panama Canal project by higher pay (three dollars a day) rioted when told to tent in a swamp. They murdered the U.S. camp chief and fled. Six hundred Germans recruited from the Hamburg waterfront mutinied and melted into the forest. Bodies of some of them turned up in fish traps below the cataracts. Spain, Portugal, and Italy soon banned emigration to the upper Madeira.

In 1910, when the line was half completed, the price of rubber peaked at $2.88 a pound—as much as $30 in 1990 money. Two years later, the Madeira–Mamoré's initial 227-mile run "from nowhere to nowhere" coincided with a plunge in prices as 8,500 tons of Malayan plantation rubber reached the market. Within a decade, Asian annual production topped 400,000 tons. When rubber prices bottomed at two and a half cents a pound, the railroad managers absconded. In 60 years of operation, the Devil's Railroad never got out of the red.

In 1971, I boarded the aging wood-burner at the upriver "nowhere," the port of Guajará-Mirím, for one of its final trips. Two bruising days later I got off at Pôrto Velho, the "nowhere" below the cataracts, a bustling hub of river, road, and air traffic. There a veteran of the 1907 to 1912 ordeal led me to the railroad hospital graveyard, grown thick with forest. We found some U.S. workers' headstones buried in shadowy humus so wet it seemed almost submarine: R. Keller, aged 21 at his death in 1909; J. R. Kennedy, died November 26, 1910, aged 26.

Months later, a new highway replaced the "Mad Mary," as the Madeira–Mamoré was known to the few elderly U.S. survivors who were still meeting annually in Falls Church, Virginia, near my home.

In 1990, at the railroad station on the Madeira riverfront, a whistle blew and a locomotive huffed and puffed alarming clouds of steam and sparks as it does every Sunday after church. With other sightseers I boarded a musty coach to ride into the past along the seven remaining miles of unkempt track. We came to a turntable, reversed the wood-burning time machine, and rode rickety-rackety back to the downstream "nowhere," now a city of 500,000 population.

Surubím, an Urueu-Wau-Wau warrior *(right)*, stands guard with bow and arrows while his betrothed, Borobá *(above)*, warms herself by a fire in the woods after a swim in a hidden pool. They are wary of rubber tappers and prospectors, interlopers from the alien world outside the forests of Rondônia who traditionally shoot them on sight.

PRECEDING PAGES: On their way to bathe in a forest pool, women of Brazil's Urueu-Wau-Wau tribe trek through a belt of savanna in the central highlands of the state of Rondônia.

Meandering in search of a downhill gradient, the Rio Purús *(left)* pursues an ever-changing course toward the Amazon mainstream in Brazil. Every year, brown floodwaters cut across peninsulas and cast off oxbow lakes that mark abandoned channels. Sediment sinks to the bottom of their quiet waters, leaving blue crescents scattered over flatland Amazonia. ¶ The Bolivia–Brazil border shifts a little whenever the Rio Guaporé *(above)* changes its course. Here the riverbed has moved little by little into Bolivia *(right)*, making about 100 minor transfers of territory to Brazil *(left)*.

Seen from the air, two pairs of scarlet macaws *(Ara macao; left)*, the most abundant of many species of giant parrots, wing over the forest. Flocks averaging ten or twelve pairs live conspicuously in trees throughout Amazonia, attracting attention with raucous calls and flashing colors. Of 40 macaws Columbus brought back from the New World, a few survived to very old age as pets in royal palaces. Early maps naming Brazil the "Land of Parrots" were decorated with paintings of macaws. ¶ Riding high on a knapsack woven of palm fronds, a scarlet macaw *(above)* seems to enjoy his status as the totemic ancestor of an Amazonian tribe. Like monkeys, pet macaws exhibit human attributes such as ostentation, spite, and mimicry. They live so long that now and then a macaw is alleged to speak the language of an extinct tribe.

It is easy to harpoon a pirarucú *(Arapaima gigas; left)* when it surfaces to gulp air. Thousands of tons of pirarucú (*paiche* in Spanish) are consumed yearly, both fresh and dried, as the main food fish of Amazonia. Its bony tongue is used for a rasp, its dried scales for sandpaper.   ¶ The *macaco-de-cheiro,* or squirrel monkey *(Saimiri sciureus; above),* is said to sleep exposed on palm leaves, a habit reflected in an Amazon fable: One night it rained and thundered and a baby macaco cried. Its father said, "Tomorrow we'll build our house." At daybreak the mother said, "Let's build the house." The father said, "Let's eat first," and they did—all day long. The next night it rained again and again the baby cried. Once more the father said, "Tomorrow we'll build our house."

An Achual tribesman in Peru drinks *masato (above)*, Amazon beer made by fermenting manioc with human saliva.   ¶ A Cofán boy in Ecuador *(right)* uses a blowgun and poisoned darts to bring down small game from the canopy.

Black stripes adorn the cheeks of the blue-and-yellow macaw *(Ara ararauna; above)*. Though native to most of Amazonia, this endangered species is less ubiquitous than the red macaw, or *canindé*—also the name of a dreaded Urueu-Wau-Wau guerrilla. Some Indians honor taboos against killing and eating macaws because of the bird's ancestral status.

Stripes tattooed on the beardless cheeks of the Urueu-Wau-Wau Indian warrior *(above)* signify that he and the macaw have a common progenitor. When his people paint themselves with the juice of genipap fruit *(Genipa americana),* the blue-black stains last only a week. For permanence, women puncture the skin artfully with a palm spine and rub in the juice.

In a confusion of colors, two great tributaries from the blue-water domain, the Xingú and the Tapajós, make their first halting contact with the Amazon. Both tributaries flow to the north, lose their velocity in terminal lakes 100 miles long and 10 miles wide, and then bend eastward through narrow exits to lose themselves in the brown-water mainstream.  ¶ The mile-wide Xingú swirl *(above)* marks the encounter at one of its several exits. The vortex is an example of "laminar shear layer behavior on a grand scale," according to specialists in fluid mechanics.  ¶ A muddy, silt-banked offshoot *(right)* of the Amazon's main channel projects into the terminal lake of the blue-water Tapajós just around the corner from Santarém, Brazil. Locals say, "The Amazon sleeps with the Tapajós," entering it at night when the river's flow predominates. But during the day, blue water escaping from the lake flows along the Santarém waterfront before merging with the Amazon.

Sailboats that ply the rivers and estuaries of the Amazon Delta region are moved by both wind and oar. Their lateen sails *(above)* recall the close-hauled caravels that first explored these waterways. Knowing their ships could tack against the wind and get back home, Portuguese captains dared to cross the Atlantic Ocean with the prevailing easterlies. In search of slaves and forest products for sale in Europe, traders penetrated a vast network of waterways on the western half of Marajó, an island as big as Switzerland in the mouth of the Amazon.

Canoes that ply swampy grasslands on the seaward half of Marajó are driven mainly by pol-
ing *(above)*. Propellor-driven craft—if settlers could afford them—might become marooned
at low water or befouled in vegetation at high water. Built by boatmen who toil at the riverine
edge of the forest covering the western half of Marajó, canoes are used for herding cattle when
waters are too deep for horses.

Only three feet above sea level in the dry season and doused with unrelenting downpours during the rainy season *(above)*, the wetlands of eastern Marajó Island seem unfit for human habitation. Yet prehistoric peoples built more than 100 great mounds that stand above encroaching fifteen-foot freshwater tides, and the ancients' magnificent pottery has survived the damp. But of the 40,000 Indians of various tribes who aligned themselves with Dutch and Portuguese armies during the European Conquest, scant traces remain.

FOLLOWING PAGES: The *pororoca* (big roar) occurs sometimes in a shallow mouth of the Amazon when a flow tide overcomes the river's force at full moon and causes an oceanic tidal bore.

AFTERWORD
AMAZONIA: TREASURE CHEST
OR PANDORA'S BOX?

# AFTERWORD
# AMAZONIA: TREASURE CHEST
# OR PANDORA'S BOX?

HE LOOKED LIKE he'd landed from Mars on a rainy day. At bay on a forest road, he faced me and brandished his powerful claws. I was amazed at his courage, for he stood only two feet tall. I had never before seen this species of anteater. It was a black tamandua capable of ripping apart a termite nest or even an intruder such as I, if I ventured too close. I snapped a picture of the outlandish fellow and then went after him with a big stick to drive him off the road. He held his ground, still facing me with open arms, almost inviting attack. I prodded and whacked him again and again until he backed away in the rain and finally retreated into the forest. I may have hurt the tamandua, but at least I saved him from workmen who might have had him for lunch.

No creature in Amazonia has had to stand up to a man for 99.9 percent of the time since the great basin was first carved out of the continent. Whereas in Africa humanity and its hominid predecessors have been part of the ecological scenery for perhaps three million years, people have arrived so recently in Amazonia that in the forest their presence is anomalous. Archaeologists estimate that Indians reached the New World less than twenty thousand years ago; Africans and Europeans have come only during the last 500 years. With the arrival of the johnny-come-latelies came the technological skill to muck up the natural order irrevocably.

Regardless of humanity, nature is always on the move in Amazonia. Climate constantly alters relationships among organisms and environments. Habitats are severely uprooted by annual flooding, periodic drought, and occurrences elsewhere on Earth such as volcanic eruptions and glaciation. It is not catastrophic natural events but the ongoing human assault on existing ecosystems, resulting in day-by-day extinction of species and possible long-term changes in world climate, that alarm people who have become aware of deforestation in Amazonia. Concern has reached so deeply in my Virginia neighborhood that a child sells homemade bracelets to help "save the Amazon forest." But most of the world's people are much more concerned with basic needs of food and shelter than with saving trees somewhere else.

The notion of saving the Amazon is new. As a voyager on the Amazon in the mid-1930s and after that with a major in Latin American Culture at the University of California, I never heard of such a thing. I studied works by nineteenth-century travelers and twentieth-century pundits who mostly extolled the wonders that hard work and modern technology could achieve in developing the region. That seemed sensible; as with most of my generation, I believed in progress. My anthropology guru, A. L. Kroeber, the dean of American anthropologists, once said, "It is pleasant to believe in progress. It makes my times and my ways superior to all others."

In the 1950s, I produced films for governments that hailed the progressive conquest of the wilderness by frontiersmen followed by dedicated educators. In the 1960s, I worked with the U.S. Agency for International Development in South America. Agency advisors taught people of Amazonian nations how to prosper with better techniques for cutting down forests, cultivating the soil, building roads and cities, and improving health and education. The goal was to approach U.S. standards of living.

No effort to "save the Amazon" can succeed without taking into account all six Amazon countries' aspirations for economic and social progress and their citizens' wishes to live as well as affluent people in other countries—brought into their lives daily on the ubiquitous TV screens. In Brazil, efforts to "save the Amazon" clash with the national policy of *Integrar para não entregar*, "Integrate lest sovereignty be lost." Brazilians at all levels of society are convinced that countries near and far would like to steal the Amazon—as if it were a tropical Antarctica up for grabs.

As soon as architect Fernando Belaúnde became president of Peru in 1962 he pushed for construction of a 4,000-mile Carretera Marginal, a highway to link the Amazon frontiers of five Andean countries: Bolivia, Peru, Ecuador, Colombia, and Venezuela. Though the road was never completed—it would have had to bridge thousands of rivers—it seemed to Brazil like a threat to its western frontier. Brazil countered by beginning the Perimetral, a highway along its northern and western perimeters. Funding collapsed when the price of imported fuel quadrupled in the 1970s. Instead, Brazil built a string of frontier airports.

Wheelers and dealers, travelers and adventurers, writers, and promoters from other nations have pestered Brazilians with countless schemes to populate and exploit its wilderness. A director of the Brazilian Army War College was quoted as having voiced in 1971 a national concern: "Only by quick action can we ensure that Amazonia will not be taken over at the end of this century by geometrically multiplying Afro-Asian nations or survivors of the apocalyptic consequences of a thermonuclear confrontation."

Although President Getulio Vargas promised in 1940 to transform Amazonia into a noble chapter in the history of civilization, little happened until Juscelino Kubitschek became president in 1956. Carrying out a campaign pledge of "50 years' progress in 5," Kubitschek immediately founded Brasília, the inland capital, to turn attention westward and relieve the pressures of a population doubling every 27 years. He rammed a road nearly to Peru, through thousands of miles of forest. Then, with increased concern for national security aroused by neighboring countries' moving into their Amazon lowland regions, the military government that took over in 1964 launched a demographic drive to the West spearheaded by the Trans-Amazon Highway. To fund development, the government offered grandiose incentives to investors. The policy led to Brazil's vaunted "economic miracle" and also to forest fires so huge they were witnessed by Gemini astronauts. The largest fire was set by Volkswagen to establish a ranch along the new Belém-Brasília Highway.

In 1967, Daniel Keith Ludwig, a supertanker tycoon born 70 years earlier in Michigan, bought a Connecticut-sized farm on the Rio Jarí to develop a pulpwood tree plantation. Ludwig had envisioned that the world information explosion would exhaust paper supplies late in the century. "I'm going to help solve the problem before I die," he told me. "I don't expect the project to turn a nickel in my lifetime." Ludwig hired teams of scientists, a succession of 26 managers, and 30,000 technicians and workers, and installed two 30,000-ton factories built in Japan and floated up the Amazon. Each day the power plant consumed 2,000 tons of waste wood and the paper pulp mill 2,000 tons of pulpwood, harvested from half a million acres of tree plantations that management claimed were self-sustaining. The plant was still operating at capacity when Ludwig died in 1989. But during all the thirteen years I observed the project, Jarí was assailed by the Brazilian press as part of a foreigner's plot to buy up the Amazon. Ludwig's close relations with his Brazilian partners and the government kept him going until a new president took office in 1982 and denied petitions to bring more factories from Japan. Ludwig walked out a billion dollars poorer. Today, a consortium of 27 Brazilian companies runs Jarí Florestal and is considering using both natural and plantation trees for charcoal needed by the steel industry.

On *National Geographic* assignments I picked up pictures of the imperiled wilderness of Amazonia and a deeper realization of the trauma of headlong development. I wondered about the loss of the greatest forest primeval on Earth. Is Amazonia a treasure chest or a Pandora's box? In the Greek myth, each of the gods conceals in a box some power to bring about the ruin of man. When in curiosity Pandora lifts the lid, out fly plagues and sorrows to afflict the world. Would that also be the worldwide repercussion of opening up Amazonia?

From 1966 to 1972, I reported on all six Amazonian nations. For my *National Geographic* article on the River Sea itself, a useful reference was the October 1971 edition of the magazine *Realidade*. Editora Abril of São Paulo, the publisher, devoted a 320-page issue to what it anticipated would be "the most important moment in the life of Amazonia, the last great natural reserve of the planet." For nine months, a team of thirteen reporters and six photographers—two of them women—roved rivers and forests, gathering material both bad and beautiful. Their interviews revealed some of the attitudes held by Brazilians heading the drive to the West:

Carlos Aloysio Weber, commander, Fifth Engineer Batallion, builders of the Pôrto Velho-Acre Highway: "When you want to do something in Amazonia, don't ask permission: just do it."

Gen. Olympia Mourao, minister of the High Military Court: "This is absurd. We're transforming the forest into a desert."

Giocondo Maria Grotti, bishop of Acre: "Health conditions are so bad that all Brazilian medical students should be obliged to do a year's service in Amazonia to earn their M.D.s."

Army Gen. Gustavo Morais, commander of the western frontier, noted for giving food and shelter to hippies floating downriver on rafts: "We're the only ones who care for settlers. When we ask help from other ministries, they send belles lettres students who descend from the plane wearing that 'save the Amazon' look on their faces. How naive."

Francisco Meirelles, 63, famous FUNAI agent, engaged—with his son Apoena, a friend of mine—in "pacifying" the Cintas Largas Indian nation: "If the government can't solve the social problems of the big urban centers, how can it solve the problem of forest Indians?"

I travel in Amazonia every year, either on assignment or on my own. Every five years I look up old friends at Km 46 along the Trans-Amazon Highway west of Altamira on the big bend of the Xingú. I first met them in 1971. Some observations I made in 1988: Cicero de Melo, a black man born in the dry Northeast, explained, "We're urbanizing. I had to sell part of my 250 acres to pay taxes."

Once blond, now gray "Gaucho" Derly Schütz and his wife Maria had pulled up stakes to move 180 Km farther west on the Trans-Amazonia. "We married off twelve of our eighteen kids and sold out for enough to pay for a smaller house and a farm with hired hands."

I found Adao Morais in Belém. In 1969, he had backpacked 2,500 road miles from Pôrto Alegre to Km 46 with his wife and two small children. "I tired of death threats from big-shot politicians who had eyes on my farm, the best around. After my son Tito took off for the big city on his motorcycle, I gave up."

Most of my current Brazilian friends live in Rondônia, a state I once knew as a magnificent tract of virgin forest. By 1991, 14.6 percent of it had been logged and burned, according to the scientist most skilled at monitoring deforestation, Philip Fearnside of the Amazon Research Institute in Manaus.

Bisecting Rondônia, highway BR-364 is a conduit for contamination of the ecosystem, like a dirty thread left in a wound. For many years after a Kubitschek crew reached Pôrto Velho by crossing corduroy causeways of logs laid in swamps, the road remained a mudhole in the wet season and a dustbin in the dry. Nobody fussed about it except colonists who emigrated from failed coffee farms and oversized families in southeastern Brazil. They built well, but at first they lacked medicines, tools, diesel oil, schoolbooks, police protection, and other amenities that usually accrue to hard-working Brazilians, but that had not reached them because the road was bad.

In the early 1980s, the World Bank paid for one-third the cost of paving the highway—for the same reasons that interstates are paved in the United States. Eighteen-wheelers soon rolled on BR-364. The road brought auto parts and paramedics to frontier towns. At peak, as many as 100,000 settlers a year trucked and bused into the state. Under dripping trees, 40,000 miners dug holes to search for cassiterite, an alluvial form of tin.

My friends the Urueu-Wau-Wau Indians live where the pristine watercourses radiate out from the center of Rondônia, surrounded by aggressors for centuries but never approached peacefully until the 1980s. They had been saved from extinction, unwittingly, by Britons who smuggled *Hevea brasiliensis* seeds out of Amazonia in the 1870s. The consequent collapse of the rubber trade allowed Indians several generations of near-respite from guerrilla war with rubber gatherers. But with BR-364 paved, the snarl of chain saws forewarned the end of their isolation. World Bank funds for medical posts and demarcation of Urueu-Wau-Wau tribal reserves evaporated. By 1990, settlers outnumbered Indians 300 to 1.

BR-364 has become a symbol of the assault on the world's rainforests. Environmentalists throughout Brazil, the United States, and western Europe, largely middle- and upper-class whites, demanded that their governments stop the World Bank from abetting the ruin of Amazonia's rainforests. Road building sputtered. No money remained for maintenance of the billion-dollar BR-364.

During the burning season in Rondônia, I asked my friend and forest guide Mauro Renato what he thought about the international outcry to protect his beloved forests. Mauro, born in 1961, had lived many years among Urueu-Wau-Wau Indians so little affected by civilization that they wore no clothes whatsoever. He is the only white man that speaks their language. He still works for the Indian agency and holds down other jobs. Mauro married an archaeologist and was visiting friends in Pôrto Velho with her and their two children. They were all dressed in Tarzan costumes for a children's party.

Mauro shook his head. "Save the forest? We can, you know. It's not too late. The vanishing species I care about most is the Indians, but FUNAI has no money, even for medicine. The boys I used to hunt with are now grown men. They go to the mines to beg for gifts."

His wife, Maria Lucia, spoke her mind. "Brazilians, especially on the frontiers, have grown up believing it was glorious to conquer the West, like the pioneers in your country. Now it seems we are doing wrong. Some of us think the real motive for stopping progress in Amazonia is to keep us underdeveloped, so you Americans can stay on top. But never mind, someday Brazil will join you up there."

But thinking of mushroom clouds of smoke towering above the forest, I demurred. "Could it be that Amazonia might be a Pandora's box?"

Maria Lucia smiled wryly; she knew the story.

When it came time to go, I was filled with *saudade*, an untranslatable Portuguese emotion composed of nostalgia, yearning, melancholy remembrance, and lost love. My frontier friends walked a few steps with me out into the smoke-reddened Rondônia sun. Charred fragments of incinerated ecosystems spun softly down from the soiled sky. Specks of ash smudged the Tarzan costumes. As I leaned to kiss her cheek, Maria Lucia recalled the conclusion of the Greek myth.

"Remember, Loren, one power remains in Pandora's box. Hope."

# LIST OF ILLUSTRATIONS

# INDEX